GLOBALVIEWPOINTS

Discrimination

Other Books of Related Interest:

At Issue Series

Child Labor and Sweatshops

Do Children Have Rights?

Racial Profiling

Transgendered People

What Rights Should Illegal Immigrants Have?

Current Controversies Series

The Elderly

Health Care

Human Genetics

Global Viewpoints Series

Death and Dying

Women's Rights

Homosexuality

Introducing Issues with Opposing Viewpoints Series

Civil Liberties

Gay Marriage

Obesity

Issues on Trial Series

Sexual Discrimination

Opposing Viewpoints Series

Gays in the Military

Obesity

Race Relations

War Crimes

GLOBALVIEWPOINTS

Discrimination

Christina Fisanick, Book Editor

GREENHAVEN PRESS
A part of Gale, Cengage Learning

GALE
CENGAGE Learning

Detroit • New York • San Francisco • New Haven, Conn • Waterville, Maine • London

Christine Nasso, *Publisher*
Elizabeth Des Chenes, *Managing Editor*

© 2011 Greenhaven Press, a part of Gale, Cengage Learning

Gale and Greenhaven Press are registered trademarks used herein under license.

For more information, contact:
Greenhaven Press
27500 Drake Rd.
Farmington Hills, MI 48331-3535
Or you can visit our Internet site at gale.cengage.com

Articles in Greenhaven Press anthologies are often edited for length to meet page requirements. In addition, original titles of these works are changed to clearly present the main thesis and to explicitly indicate the author's opinion. Every effort is made to ensure that Greenhaven Press accurately reflects the original intent of the authors. Every effort has been made to trace the owners of copyrighted material.

Cover image copyright © iWitness Photos/Alamy.

LIBRARY OF CONGRESS CATALOGING-IN-PUBLICATION DATA

Discrimination / Christina Fisanick, book editor.
   p. cm. -- (Global viewpoints)
   Includes bibliographical references and index.
   ISBN 978-0-7377-5189-5 (hardcover) -- ISBN 978-0-7377-5190-1 (pbk.)
   1. Discrimination. I. Fisanick, Christina.
   HM821.D565 2011
   305--dc22

                                                           2011006258

Printed in the United States of America

ACC LIBRARY SERVICES AUSTIN, TX

Contents

Chapter 2: Gender and Sexuality Discrimination

Chapter 3: Racial and Ethnic Discrimination

Caste discrimination still plays a role in the everyday lives of Indian people, including schoolchildren who are often forced to do menial jobs at school.

Chapter 4: Cultural and Religious Discrimination

Foreword

*"The problems of all of humanity can
only be solved by all of humanity."*
—Swiss author Friedrich Dürrenmatt

Global interdependence has become an undeniable reality.
Mass media and technology have increased worldwide
access to information and created a society of global citizens.
Understanding and navigating this global community is a
challenge, requiring a high degree of information literacy and
a new level of learning sophistication.

Building on the success of its flagship series, *Opposing
Viewpoints*, Greenhaven Press has created the *Global Viewpoints* series to examine a broad range of current, often con-
troversial topics of worldwide importance from a variety of
international perspectives. Providing students and other readers with the information they need to explore global connec-
tions and think critically about worldwide implications, each
Global Viewpoints volume offers a panoramic view of a topic
of widespread significance.

Drugs, famine, immigration—a broad, international treatment is essential to do justice to social, environmental, health,
and political issues such as these. Junior high, high school,
and early college students, as well as general readers, can all
use *Global Viewpoints* anthologies to discern the complexities
relating to each issue. Readers will be able to examine unique
national perspectives while, at the same time, appreciating the
interconnectedness that global priorities bring to all nations
and cultures.

Material in each volume is selected from a diverse range of
sources, including journals, magazines, newspapers, nonfiction
books, speeches, government documents, pamphlets, organiza-

tion newsletters, and position papers. *Global Viewpoints* is truly global, with material drawn primarily from international sources available in English and secondarily from US sources with extensive international coverage.

Features of each volume in the *Global Viewpoints* series include:

- An **annotated table of contents** that provides a brief summary of each essay in the volume, including the name of the country or area covered in the essay.

- An **introduction** specific to the volume topic.

- A **world map** to help readers locate the countries or areas covered in the essays.

- For each viewpoint, an **introduction** that contains notes about the author and source of the viewpoint explains why material from the specific country is being presented, summarizes the main points of the viewpoint, and offers three **guided reading questions** to aid in understanding and comprehension.

- **For further discussion** questions that promote critical thinking by asking the reader to compare and contrast aspects of the viewpoints or draw conclusions about perspectives and arguments.

- A worldwide list of **organizations to contact** for readers seeking additional information.

- A **periodical bibliography** for each chapter and a **bibliography of books** on the volume topic to aid in further research.

- A comprehensive **subject index** to offer access to people, places, events, and subjects cited in the text, with the countries covered in the viewpoints highlighted.

Global Viewpoints is designed for a broad spectrum of readers who want to learn more about current events, history, political science, government, international relations, economics, environmental science, world cultures, and sociology— students doing research for class assignments or debates, teachers and faculty seeking to supplement course materials, and others wanting to understand current issues better. By presenting how people in various countries perceive the root causes, current consequences, and proposed solutions to worldwide challenges, *Global Viewpoints* volumes offer readers opportunities to enhance their global awareness and their knowledge of cultures worldwide.

Introduction

"In the end antiblack, antifemale, and all forms of discrimination are equivalent to the same thing—antihumanism."

Shirley Chisholm,
Unbought and Unbossed, 1970

Despite social and legal changes, discrimination remains a problem in societies around the world. People can be discriminated against based on their age, race, ethnicity, gender, sexual orientation, ability, class, religion, and many other characteristics. In addition, it can be subtle or overt, and discrimination can take place in the home, in the workplace, and even in a nation's laws. Throughout history, different groups have been targets of systematic discrimination, and the remedies for ending this sometimes fatal treatment has varied according to culture. Unfortunately, the last century gave rise to some of the worst cases of discrimination in human history.

Partly because disorders of the brain have been little understood until recently, people across the globe have struggled with how to treat individuals with mental disorders such as schizophrenia, epilepsy, and retardation. As a result, mentally ill persons have faced severe discrimination for centuries. Fear of passing on mental disabilities to offspring led to the forced sterilization of mentally ill persons across the globe through the early to middle twentieth century. These sterilizations were sanctioned by world governments and carried out without consent. The most famous compulsory sterilization program was undertaken in Germany during the Nazi regime. In July 1933 Adolf Hitler passed the Law for the Prevention of Hereditarily Diseased Offspring, which resulted in the forced sterilization of four hundred thousand people by the end of World War II, according to Ian Kershaw in *Hitler*.

Hitler's discrimination and cruelty did not stop with the mentally disabled. Under his rule, he exterminated six hundred thousand people of Jewish descent during the Holocaust. Sometimes discrimination even occurs within a religious group, as was the case in Hinduism. Members of the lowest caste, or untouchables, were shunned in Indian culture until the 1950s when changes were made to the Indian constitution that abolished the caste system. However, India's lowest class, also referred to as dalits, remain targets of discriminatory practices. In his December 5, 2010, article on ChristianPost .com, Charles Boyd argues, "Dalits face being attacked or physically abused and are often forced to undertake the worst jobs." The plight of the dalits demonstrates the challenge that governments and their citizens face when trying to stop deeply rooted discriminatory practices.

Similar to the dalits, people with leprosy have faced discrimination for hundreds of years. Leprosy, or Hansen's disease, is a disease that affects the nervous system and upper respiratory tract, but most people fear acquiring it due to the skin deformities it causes. Throughout history, lepers have been treated like second-class citizens and often forced to live in exile. Not only have lepers been castigated because of the fear of the spread of the disease, they have also been shunned because of the association between the disease and moral decay. In 1951 Japanese citizen Matsuo Fujimoto was accused of murder and then hanged in 1962. He was a leper, and many people argued that he was wrongfully convicted because of the judge and jury's prejudices against lepers. In March 2005 the Verification Committee Concerning Hansen's Disease, which was formed to investigate claims of discrimination against lepers, concluded that Fujimoto was not given a fair trial and that his conviction was unconstitutional. Today, it is against the law in nearly all countries to discriminate against persons with leprosy, but such individuals continue to be shunned in many cultures.

Unfortunately, no matter how far a culture evolves, it seems that groups of people are always pushed to the bottom of the social hierarchy. Women have played that role for centuries in most societies. Women have been discriminated against in government, in health care, and in just about all realms of society. Although the plight of women has improved in the last fifty years, a gap remains between the way men and women are treated, including in terms of pay, employment opportunities, and other workplace issues. A 2004 report published on China.org notes that "some [non-state-owned-enterprises] terminate job contracts of pregnant women in order to avoid covering medical fees or providing maternity leave. It is not unheard of for an enterprise's contract to contain a clause forbidding pregnancy." And this type of discrimination is not limited to China. Reports of prejudice against pregnant women in the workplace are common in other parts of Asia, South America, and North America.

In addition to the social ramifications of discrimination, systematic prejudice can lead to wide-scale consequences such as rape and death. For example, after decades of discrimination, genocide began in Rwanda in 1994. Belgian colonists and other groups, including the Catholic Church, had long established the Tutsi ethnic group as the preferred peoples, largely because of what was believed to be their European heritage. After years of facing prejudice, the other major ethnic group in Rwanda, the Hutu, rebelled and began producing propaganda about the Tutsis. According to a report by the Human Rights Council, "The Hutu remembered past years of oppressive Tutsi rule, and many of them not only resented but also feared the minority." In the end, an estimated eight hundred thousand Tutsi and peace-supporting Hutu were murdered by their friends and neighbors.

Discrimination is not always so overt, which makes it difficult for victims to seek justice. Proving any kind of discrimination is challenging because many decisions that are made based on prejudice are not announced. For example, if a supervisor asks a group of workers out for a business luncheon and the only one not invited is of a different race, it might be construed as racist. Even in cultures where overt discrimination is illegal and socially unacceptable, subtle discrimination can still exist. For instance, according to an article by Edward Telles in the September 2007 issue of the *UN Chronicle*, "Most discrimination in Brazil is subtle and includes slights, aggressions and numerous other informal practices, while consciously egregious and overt racism directed at particular individuals, especially in the form of racial insults, is more commonly recognized as racist." The consequences of this form of discrimination might even be more severe because they are difficult to prove and to correct.

Despite the grim history of global discrimination, humanity is trying to right its wrongs by passing stronger legislation and by better understanding the toll that discrimination and prejudice play on individuals and society as a whole. Recent attempts by the United Nations to get all world governments to adopt the Convention on the Elimination of All Forms of Discrimination Against Women is a step toward such societal reconciliation. The authors in *Global Viewpoints: Discrimination* debate current views on the subject in the following chapters: "Health Discrimination," "Gender and Sexuality Discrimination," "Racial and Ethnic Discrimination," and "Cultural and Religious Discrimination." These viewpoints reveal the detrimental effect of discrimination on victims as well as on perpetrators.

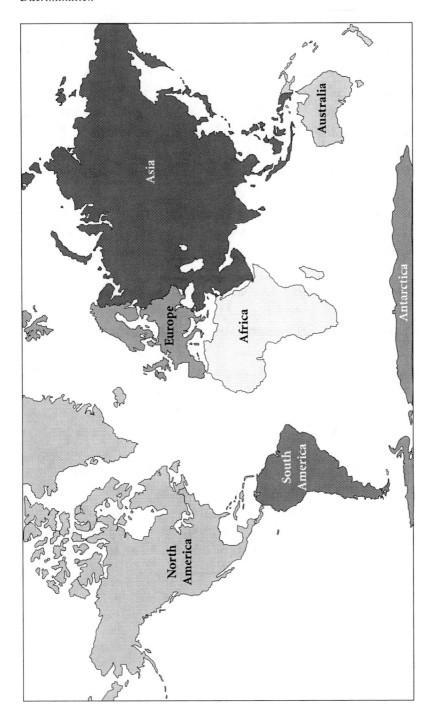

GLOBAL VIEWPOINTS

CHAPTER 1

Health Discrimination

Britain's National Health Service Discriminates Against Older Citizens

Alasdair Palmer

Alasdair Palmer is a contributor to the Spectator, *as well as a columnist and the public policy editor for the* Telegraph. *In the following viewpoint, Palmer discusses some cases of fatal neglect of elderly people in British hospitals. Some of these cases involved people admitted with nonterminal conditions, but who nevertheless died in the hospital. Palmer suggests that such treatment of older people is institutionalized by insufficient funding for care of the elderly and by the quality-adjusted life year (QALY) system that determines the use of medical resources on individuals by estimating how many years of high-quality life they have remaining. Since elderly people don't have many years of life left, their QALY scores tend to be lower, and so the elderly are often not given priority treatment.*

As you read, consider the following questions:

1. How long did it take for Barbara Yeo, who was admitted for constipation, to be placed on the hostpital's "do not resuscitate" list?

2. As explained by the author, what abuses of elderly people did BBC's *Panorama* expose with the help of a hidden camera placed by one of the nurses?

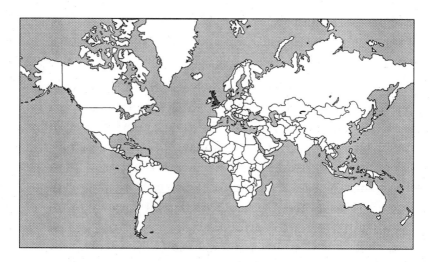

3. How much of NHS's budget is allocated to care for the elderly? What percentage of patients in hospital wards are over 65?

Many people with elderly or terminally ill relatives have had to confront the issue of whether it would be better if some way could be found to hasten their sick relative's death. Informal arrangements exist for hastening death within the Health Service. They often take the form of increasing the dosage of painkillers to the point where it will relieve the agony—and also ensure death. That's what happened in my mother's case. She had terminal and untreatable cancer. Her wishes were clear: she did not want to go on living in agonising pain. The doctors and nurses were equally clear about what was going to happen if her dose of painkillers was increased to the point where her pain ceased: she would die faster than she otherwise would. Her dose of morphine was increased. She died peacefully soon afterwards.

That seems to me to be the acceptable—indeed the right—way for doctors and nurses to hasten death. Unfortunately, it does not seem to be the only, or even the most common, way in which they actually do it. The experience of taking an elderly relative to hospital and finding that he or she is treated in a way which causes both pain and harm is frighteningly common.

Barbara Yeo is one example of that trend. She was an 83-year-old woman who was admitted to hospital in March this year [2005] for what was thought to be constipation. Within a week, Mrs Yeo was on the hospital's 'do not resuscitate' list. No terminal illness had been diagnosed. Her family found out by chance. 'I was having a conversation with one of the doctors,' Harriet Yeo, Barbara Yeo's daughter, explained to me, 'in which I wanted to ensure that all steps would be taken to resuscitate her if at any point she should lose consciousness. The doctor told me outright that he didn't agree with that. He didn't think she should be resuscitated. He added insouciantly that, nevertheless, he would "seek a second opinion on that topic".'

Since other doctors involved with her mother's care took the same attitude, that was not reassuring. 'One of them asked me, "How do you know she wants to live?" The real question was how he knew she wanted to die! I knew she wanted to live because she had said so dozens of times.' Harriet Yeo remembers that the doctor had insisted that he was 'qualified to judge quality of life'. The clear implication was that Harriet Yeo was not, and nor was her mother. The 'medical team' then exposed her to infection by bringing on to her ward another patient with a highly infectious bug. Mrs Yeo duly caught that bug. It killed her within a few days. And yet, Harriet Yeo insists, she had gone into that hospital as a woman of perfectly sound mind and reasonably functioning body; certainly she had nothing approaching any kind of terminal illness. Harriet Yeo was so incensed by what happened to her mother that she has started Forgetmenot, a charity whose purpose is to try to ensure that the elderly are properly treated. She has been overwhelmed with people complaining that their elderly relatives had their pain prolonged and their illnesses worsened by medical neglect. Those cases include Charles Andrews, who was apparently left in terrible, unnecessary agony for two months because no one bothered to look at his test results; and John Williams, an 88-year-old who was admitted to hospital after being diagnosed as suffering from 'acute peritonitis'. Mr Williams was told he had three days to live and given no treatment. A second doctor gave him a final examination, and concluded he did not have peritonitis, just a gallstone, and his life was not in danger. But in hospital Mr Williams acquired an infection. The infection killed him. Mr Williams's death, like Mr Andrews's, will make an appearance in NHS [National Health Service] statistics. The neglect responsible for it will not.

The failure to treat elderly people properly is sufficiently frequent to suggest that it results from a deliberate policy. When the BBC's *Panorama* persuaded a nurse in an acute ward to use a hidden camera earlier this year, all the instances of neglect she recorded happened to old people: elderly patients were left in excruciating pain because of a failure properly to administer their pain medication; their food was eaten by medical staff; nurses ignored their cries for help; and some elderly patients even died without anyone noticing what had happened.

Health care resources, as we all know, are not infinite: they have to be rationed somehow. The usual basis for making rationing decisions used by organisations such as the National Institute for [Health and] Clinical Excellence (Nice), which decides what medicines the NHS should buy, is 'Quality Adjusted Life Years', or Qalys. Treatments are ranked by their outcomes in terms of how many years of high-quality life they will give to their beneficiaries. Qalys do not favour old people: they do not have many years left, their score drops even lower when those years are adjusted for 'quality'. One effect of using Qalys may be that old people drop down the list of doctors' and nurses' priorities: they are, as I once heard one hard-pressed nurse say, 'all going to die soon anyway'. And if you are at the bottom of the list made by people who feel too busy even to look after those at the top of it, your chances of being properly cared for collapse.

A second doctor gave him a final examination, and con-cluded he did not have peritonitis, just a gallstone, and his life was not in danger. But in hospital Mr Williams acquired an infection. The infection killed him.

The government denies this. Health ministers point to the fact that the NHS has a National Director for Older People services, Professor Ian Philp, whose brief is to 'stamp out age-ism in the NHS'. They also insist that nearly half the NHS's total budget is spent on people over the age of 65. Which is true. The trouble is, two-thirds of patients in hospital wards are over 65. Since hospital care is by far the most expensive part of the NHS, you would expect at least two-thirds of it to go on the over-65 age group.

It doesn't. It may be that minimising treatment for the old is the most rational way to allocate the resources we have. The more brutal health economists argue that it just isn't worth expending too large a slice of scarce medical care on them; it means that those who have more to look forward to, who have not already had a chance to live a long life and who score high on Qalys, are denied it.

It is not a policy which ministers will admit to following. But perhaps they do—and perhaps they are right. But it surely cannot be right that old people should be so cruelly neglected in the way they frequently seem to be at present. To live for ever is not something anyone can reasonably demand. But the NHS certainly has the resources to ensure that everyone in Britain can die without pain and with a modicum of dignity. It is a monumental scandal that its resources are not being used to produce that result.

HIV and AIDS Discrimination and Stigma

AVERT

AVERT is a United Kingdom–based, international nonprofit organization that works to avert HIV and AIDS worldwide, through education, treatment, and care. In the following viewpoint, AVERT explores the issue of stigma and discrimination of persons suffering from HIV and AIDS. Such discrimination can come in the form of government policies targeted at persons living with the virus to families and communities shunning sufferers. AVERT is concerned mostly with how these various types of discrimination impact the treatment of patients.

As you read, consider the following questions:

1. According to a 2010 UNAIDS report, what percentage of countries have legislation that protects people with HIV from discrimination?

2. Approximately how many countries have placed restrictions on people with HIV or AIDS during long-term stays of more than ninety days?

3. By the end of 2009, how many people were living with HIV around the globe?

HIV and AIDS Stigma and Discrimination

AIDS-related stigma and discrimination refers to prejudice, negative attitudes, abuse and maltreatment directed at people living with HIV and AIDS. They can result in being shunned by family, peers and the wider community; poor treatment in healthcare and education settings; an erosion of rights; psychological damage; and can negatively affect the success of testing and treatment.

AIDS stigma and discrimination exist worldwide, although they manifest themselves differently across countries, communities, religious groups and individuals. They occur alongside other forms of stigma and discrimination, such as racism, homophobia or misogyny and can be directed towards those involved in what are considered socially unacceptable activities such as prostitution or drug use.

Stigma not only makes it more difficult for people trying to come to terms with HIV and manage their illness on a personal level, but it also interferes with attempts to fight the AIDS epidemic as a whole. On a national level, the stigma associated with HIV can deter governments from taking fast, effective action against the epidemic, whilst on a personal level it can make individuals reluctant to access HIV testing, treatment and care.

UN [United Nations] Secretary-General Ban Ki-moon says:

> Stigma remains the single most important barrier to public action. It is a main reason why too many people are afraid to see a doctor to determine whether they have the disease, or to seek treatment if so. It helps make AIDS the silent killer, because people fear the social disgrace of speaking about it, or taking easily available precautions. Stigma is a chief reason why the AIDS epidemic continues to devastate societies around the world. . . .

Types of HIV/AIDS–Related Stigma and Discrimination

AIDS-related stigma can lead to discrimination such as negative treatment and denied opportunities on the basis of their HIV status. This discrimination can occur at all levels of a

for the last appointment of the day last week, they covered the chair, the light, the doctors were wearing three pairs of gloves...."

A review of research into stigma in healthcare settings advocated a multi-pronged approach to tackling it, requiring action on the individual, environmental and policy levels. Healthcare workers need to be made aware of the negative effect that stigma can have on the quality of care patients receive; they should have accurate information about the risk of HIV infection, the misperception of which can lead to stigmatising actions; and they should also be encouraged to not associate HIV with immoral behaviour. Facilities should have sufficient equipment and information so health workers can carry out universal precautions and prevent exposure to HIV.

Policies within healthcare settings can also be effective in reducing stigma. Such programmes would involve participatory methods like role play and group discussion, as well as training on stigma and universal precautions. The involvement of people living with HIV could lead to a greater understanding of patients' needs and the negative effect of stigma.

Healthcare workers need to be made aware of the negative effect that stigma can have on the quality of care patients receive....

Employment Discrimination

In the workplace, people living with HIV may suffer stigma from their co-workers and employers, such as social isolation and ridicule, or experience discriminatory practices, such as termination or refusal of employment. Fear of an employer's reaction can cause a person living with HIV anxiety:

"It is always in the back of your mind, if I get a job, should I tell my employer about my HIV status? There is a fear of how they will react to it. It may cost you your job, it may make you so uncomfortable it changes relationships. Yet you would want to be able to explain about why you are absent, and going to the doctors." HIV-positive woman UK ...

Restrictions on Travel and Stay

Many countries have laws that restrict the entry, stay and residence of people living with HIV.

As of December 2010, people living with HIV were subject to restrictions during long-term stays (more than 90 days) in sixty-five countries and of these, 18 also applied restrictions during short-term stays. Restrictions for short-term stays include the need to disclose HIV status or to be subject to a mandatory HIV test.

It is reported that around thirty countries including Egypt, Russia, and Singapore deported foreigners based on their positive status alone.

Many countries have laws that restrict the entry, stay and residence of people living with HIV.

Some countries have policies that could violate confidentiality of status if, for example, a stamp is required on a waiver or passport in order to gain entry or stay. Students living with HIV are barred from applying to study in certain countries including Malaysia and Syria.

Until the 4th of January 2010 the United States restricted all HIV-positive people from entering the country, whether they were on holiday or visiting on a longer-term basis.

A database maintained by the German AIDS Federation, the European AIDS Treatment Group and the International AIDS Society, presents updated information on such travel restrictions (if there are any) in 196 countries: www.hivtravel .org.

Deportation of people living with HIV has potentially life-threatening consequences if they have been taking antiretrovi-

Why Is There Stigma Related to HIV and AIDS?

Fear of contagion coupled with negative, value-based assumptions about people who are infected leads to high levels of stigma surrounding HIV and AIDS.

Factors that contribute to HIV/AIDS–related stigma:

- HIV/AIDS is a life-threatening disease, and therefore people react to it in strong ways.

- HIV infection is associated with behaviours (such as homosexuality, drug addiction, prostitution or promiscuity) that are already stigmatised in many societies.

- Most people become infected with HIV through sex which often carries moral baggage.

- There is a lot of inaccurate information about how HIV is transmitted, creating irrational behaviour and misperceptions of personal risk.

- HIV infection is often thought to be the result of personal irresponsibility.

- Religious or moral beliefs lead some people to believe that being infected with HIV is the result of moral fault (such as promiscuity or 'deviant sex') that deserves to be punished.

AVERT, "HIV and AIDS Discrimination and Stigma,"
May 26, 2010. www.avert.org.

ral drugs. If they are deported to a country that has limited treatment provision, this could lead to drug resistance and death. Alternatively, people living with HIV may face deportation to a country where they would be subject to even further discrimination. As Human Rights Watch has pointed out, this practice could contravene international law.

Community-level stigma and discrimination can manifest as ostracism, rejection and verbal and physical abuse.

Community Discrimination

Community-level stigma and discrimination towards people living with HIV/AIDS is found all over the world. A community's reaction to somebody living with HIV/AIDS can have a huge effect on that person's life. If the reaction is hostile a person may be ostracised and discriminated against and may be forced to leave their home, or change their daily activities such as shopping, socialising or schooling.

> "At first relations with the local school were wonderful and Michael thrived there. Only the head teacher and Michael's personal class assistant knew of his illness.... Then someone broke the confidentiality and told a parent that Michael had AIDS. That parent, of course, told all the others. This caused such panic and hostility that we were forced to move out of the area. Michael was no longer welcome at the school. Other children were not allowed to play with him— instead they jeered and taunted him cruelly. One day a local mother started screaming at us to keep him away from her children and shouting that he should have been put down at birth.... Ignorance about HIV means that people are frightened. And frightened people do not behave rationally. We could well be driven out of our home yet again." British woman describing the experience of her foster son in a British school

Community-level stigma and discrimination can manifest as ostracism, rejection and verbal and physical abuse. It has even extended to murder. AIDS-related murders have been reported in countries as diverse as Brazil, Colombia, Ethiopia,

India, South Africa and Thailand. In December 1998, Gugu Dhlamini was stoned and beaten to death by neighbours in her township near Durban, South Africa, after speaking openly on World AIDS Day about her HIV status. It is therefore not surprising that 79 percent of people living with HIV who participated in a global study, feared social discrimination following their status disclosure.

Family Discrimination

In the majority of developing countries families are the primary caregivers when somebody falls ill. There is clear evidence that families play an important role in providing support and care for people living with HIV and AIDS. However, not all family responses are positive. HIV-infected members of the family can find themselves stigmatised and discriminated against within the home. There is concern that women and non-heterosexual family members are more likely than children and men to be mistreated.

> "When I was in hospital, my father came once. Then he shouted that I had AIDS. Everyone could hear. He said: this is AIDS, she's a victim. With my brother and his wife I wasn't allowed to eat from the same plates, I got a plastic cup and plates and I had to sleep in the kitchen. I was not even allowed to play with the kids." HIV-positive woman, Zimbabwe

A Dutch survey of people living with HIV found that stigma in family settings—in particular avoidance, exaggerated kindness and being told to conceal one's status—was a significant predictor of psychological distress. This was believed to be due to the absence of unconditional love and support, which families are expected to provide. Furthermore, people living with HIV are often worried about losing family and friends if they disclose their status. As a global study illustrated, 35 percent of those interviewed cited this as a concern surrounding disclosure.

The Way Forward

HIV-related stigma and discrimination severely hamper efforts to effectively fight the HIV and AIDS epidemic. Fear of discrimination often prevents people from seeking treatment for AIDS or from admitting their HIV status publicly. People with (or suspected of having) HIV may be turned away from healthcare services and employment, or refused entry to a foreign country. In some cases, they may be forced from home by their families and rejected by their friends and colleagues. The stigma attached to HIV/AIDS can extend to the next generation, placing an emotional burden on those left behind.

Denial goes hand in hand with discrimination, with many people continuing to deny that HIV exists in their communities. Today, HIV/AIDS threatens the welfare and well-being of people throughout the world. At the end of the 2009, 33.3 million people were living with HIV with 1.8 million having died from AIDS-related illness that year. Combating stigma and discrimination against people who are affected by HIV/AIDS is a vital ingredient for preventing and controlling the global epidemic.

HIV-related stigma and discrimination severely hamper efforts to effectively fight the HIV and AIDS epidemic.

So how can progress be made in overcoming this stigma and discrimination? How can we change people's attitudes to AIDS? A certain amount can be achieved through the legal process. In some countries people living with HIV lack knowledge of their rights in society. They need to be educated, so they are able to challenge the discrimination, stigma and denial that they encounter. Institutional and other monitoring mechanisms can enforce the rights of people with HIV and provide powerful means of mitigating the worst effects of discrimination and stigma.

"We can fight stigma. Enlightened laws and policies are key. But it begins with openness, the courage to speak out. Schools should teach respect and understanding. Religious leaders should preach tolerance. The media should condemn prejudice and use its influence to advance social change, from securing legal protections to ensuring access to health care." Ban Ki-moon, secretary-general of the United Nations

However, no policy or law can alone combat HIV/AIDS–related discrimination. Stigma and discrimination will continue to exist so long as societies as a whole have a poor understanding of HIV and AIDS and the pain and suffering caused by negative attitudes and discriminatory practices. The fear and prejudice that lie at the core of the HIV/AIDS discrimination need to be tackled at the community and national levels, with AIDS education playing a crucial role. A more enabling environment needs to be created to increase the visibility of people with HIV/AIDS as a 'normal' part of any society. The presence of treatment makes this task easier; where there is hope, people are less afraid of AIDS; they are more willing to be tested for HIV, to disclose their status and to seek care if necessary. In the future, the task is to confront the fear-based messages and biased social attitudes, in order to reduce the discrimination and stigma of people living with HIV and AIDS.

In Senegal, Children with Mental Illnesses Suffer Discrimination

IRIN

IRIN is the humanitarian news and analysis service of the United Nations Office for the Coordination of Humanitarian Affairs. This report does not necessarily reflect the views of the United Nations. In the following viewpoint, the author reports on how children with mental or neurological disorders are treated in Senegal. The attitude of people in general is that such children are abnormal, possessed, or a punishment from God. Parents try to hide these children, and fathers often abandon the child and home. There is only one public school to care for the education of children with such disorders, and often it must turn away new applicants because it cannot meet the demand. Most teachers on staff are not trained to care for or educate children with mental disorders. The state does not have facilities to train teachers on how to care and educate children with mental disorders. Five private institutions provide care for those who can afford it.

As you read, consider the following questions:

1. According to the author, how many people in Africa have unipolar depressive disorders? Epilepsy? Bipolar affective disorder? Schizophrenia?

IRIN, "Senegal: Children with Disability—When Stigma Means Abandonment," IRIN, August 11, 2010. Reproduced by permission.

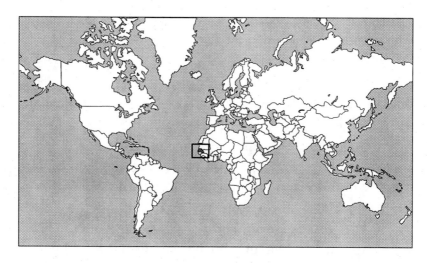

2. According to the author, what is the name of Senegal's public school for children with mental and neurological disorders, and how many new applicants did it receive in 2009? How many did it turn away?

3. What does Claude Sarr, director of the Aminata Mbaye Centre for mentally disabled young people, think will lead to better training and facilities for these children?

In Senegal many women refuse to take mentally disabled children on public transport; families hide children with mental or neurological disorders, and some parents disown them outright. Such is the stigma of having a child with these widely misunderstood illnesses.

"In Senegal people simply regard children with such conditions as 'abnormal', whatever the disability—mental or physical," said Ngor Ndour, a psychologist specializing in mental disorders in children.

"While it might be somewhat simpler to explain that a child is deaf, it is complicated to explain mental disorders because people automatically see a mystical aspect—the child is 'abnormal', possessed, half-man, half-animal," said Ndour, a former director of Senegal's only public school for children with mental and neurological disorders.

The World Health Organization (WHO) notes that around the globe people with mental disorders and neurological conditions like epilepsy face discrimination and rights violations.

According to the latest WHO global burden of disease statistics, from 2004, 13.4 million people in Africa had unipolar depressive disorders, 7.7 million epilepsy, 2.7 million bipolar affective disorder and 2.1 million schizophrenia.

Ndour said in many cases the mother thinks a mentally disabled child is her fault, and the father often flees. This is what happened to Mariama Bodian, mother of Seynabou, an eight-year-old girl simply described by her mother as "psychotic".

The World Health Organization (WHO) notes that around the globe people with mental disorders and neurological conditions like epilepsy face discrimination and rights violations.

"[Her father] left us as soon as he knew the child had a mental disability—she was four months old," Bodian told IRIN. "We have not heard from him since."

In the small rented room in the capital, Dakar, where she lives with Seynabou, Bodian said: "The father did not come to terms with our daughter's disorder. He does not help us financially—he no longer communicates with us."

Astou Ndong is also raising two sons alone because her husband left when Abdoulaye, who has epilepsy and is now 11, was born. "[The father] was ashamed of Abdoulaye and told me to go to the village with him so we could hide the child," she told IRIN.

"But I didn't want to. I love my child, I want to help him, and I knew that for school and healthcare he would be better off here in the city," Ndong said. Her refusal meant her husband sends them no money, and she earns a meagre living as a trader.

Curse, Punishment

The shame attached to mental and neurological disorders is a strong force, said Dakar hairdresser Ibrahim Gueye, the father of a child with a severe learning disability.

"In Senegalese society it is quite difficult to have a child with a mental disorder. The prevailing belief is that it is a curse; it is difficult to get family and friends to accept such a child."

Another common belief is that the mother was unfaithful in the marriage, and a child with such a condition is a punishment from God, said Dominique Ndeki, director of the Education and Training Centre for the Mentally Disabled (CEFDI), Senegal's only public school for these children.

Ndeki said one day a family brought a six-year-old boy to register at CEFDI. "They told me it was the first time he had been out of the house; they had been hiding him."

Hiding mentally ill children is common, and may even be an improvement over the past. Ndeki recalled hearing stories, when he was a boy, of mentally disabled children deliberately being drowned.

Capacity

Both Seynabou and Abdoulaye attend CEFDI, and although the city offers more by way of education and healthcare than the rural areas, facilities are still inadequate.

The education ministry has no national statistics on the number of mentally handicapped children, but Ndeki said in 2009 CEFDI had to turn away 54 of the 81 children who applied from all over the country because the facility could not accommodate any more new students. When registration for the 2010–11 academic year opened, 20 families came to register children in just two days.

Action to Support People with Mental Illness

Empowerment has been described as the opposite of self-stigmatisation. Policy makers can provide specific financial support for ways in which individuals with mental illness can empower themselves or be empowered. Such specific support might include:

- Promoting participation in formulating care plans and crisis plans for people with mental illness.

- Providing cognitive-behavioural therapy for people with mental illness to reverse negative self-stigma.

- Running regular assessments of consumer satisfaction with services.

- Creating user-led and user-run services.

- Developing peer-support worker roles in mainstream mental health care.

- Encouraging employers to give positive credit for experience of mental illness.

- Enabling people with mental illness to take part in treatment and service evaluation and research.

Graham Thornicroft et al.,
"Reducing Stigma and Discrimination:
Candidate Interventions,"
International Journal of Mental Health Systems,
vol. 2, no. 3, 2008.

Senegal has five private institutions for mentally handicapped children—four in Dakar and one in the northern city of Saint Louis—but many families cannot afford them.

CEFDI, which takes children with Down's syndrome, epilepsy, and a variety of other disorders, has two specialists and three other teachers, who have not been trained to teach mentally or neurologically disabled children, to educate 109 students from four to 20 years old, according to Ndeki.

Saliou Sène, an elementary school superintendent, said there were plans to train teachers in the care and education of mentally disabled children; the education ministry said at present Senegal had no facilities to provide such training.

Claude Sarr, director of the Aminata Mbaye Centre for mentally disabled young people, a private centre, said better facilities and training were linked to broader acceptance on the part of families with affected children.

"Awareness is difficult, but little by little it's improving," he said. "Parents [of these children] must mobilize to help raise awareness among the authorities."

Discrimination Against Obese Americans Is a Threat to Their Health

Daniel Engber

Daniel Engber is a senior editor at Slate, *a daily web-based magazine that offers popular culture analysis and political commentary. In the following viewpoint, he argues that the current war on the obesity epidemic in the United States is making the problem worse. By discriminating against obese people, health care professionals and society in general are intensifying the negative side effects of being overweight because anti-fat bias can cause stress. Engber asserts that there are better ways rather than hatred to address the needs of obese Americans.*

As you read, consider the following questions:

1. According to Engber, what percentage wage penalty do women who are at least sixty-four pounds overweight suffer?

2. By how much has the prevalence of weight discrimination increased since the mid-1990s, as cited by the author?

3. In which state is it illegal for employers to discriminate on the basis of body size?

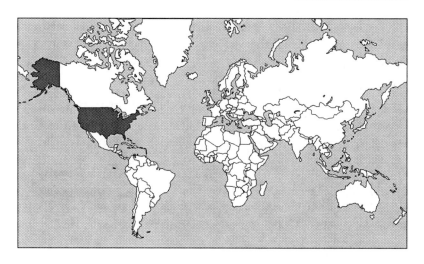

Just about every discussion of obesity and health care begins with same purported fact: The diseases associated with excess weight are impoverishing the nation with $147 billion in unnecessary medical bills every year. In my last column ("Give Us Your Tired, Your Poor, Your Big Fat Asses . . ."), I argued that obesity can also make us poor individually, since fat people face rampant discrimination on the job and marriage markets.

A recent paper from Yale's Rudd Center for Food Policy & Obesity hints at the scope of this anti-fat prejudice. We know, for example, that if you're fat, you make less money. Lots of studies have shown how body size plays out in the working world: According to one, women who are two standard deviations (or 64 pounds) overweight suffer a wage penalty of 9 percent (PDF); another found that severely obese white women lose out on one-quarter of their potential income. There's also evidence that obese women are less likely to attend college or maintain romantic relationships, even controlling for socioeconomic background. (One survey found that a few extra pounds could reduce a woman's chance of getting married by 20 percent.)

Heavy people may face discrimination in medical settings, too. The authors of the review, Rebecca Puhl and Chelsea Heuer, cite numerous surveys of anti-fat attitudes among health care workers, who tend to see obese patients as ugly, lazy, weak-willed, and lacking in motivation to improve their health. Doctors describe treating fatties as a waste of time, and the staff at teaching hospitals appear to single them out for derogatory jokes. Unsurprisingly, many obese people avoid seeing their primary care providers altogether, and those who do are less likely to be screened for breast, cervical, and colorectal cancers. (That's true even among those with health insurance and college degrees.)

Mental anguish harms the body; weight stigma can break your heart.

These data points suggest a rather simple approach to America's obesity problem: Stop hating. If we weren't such unrepentant body bigots, fat people might earn more money, stay in school, and receive better medical care in hospitals and doctors' offices. All that would go a long way toward mitigating the health effects of excess weight—and its putative costs. But there's an even better reason to think that America's glutton intolerance is a threat to public health and the federal budget. Recent epidemiological research implies that the shame of being obese poses its own medical risk. Mental anguish harms the body; weight stigma can break your heart.

The victims of chronic stress or depression, whatever their size, tend to maintain higher levels of certain inflammatory chemicals in their bloodstream. Under normal circumstances—and over the short term—these cytokines help to control the body's response to dangerous situations like injury or illness. The chemicals create their own problems, though, when they stick around too long. A sustained or elevated stress response seems to increase your risk of heart disease, hypertension, and diabetes. That may explain some of the relationships between health and wealth: Blood tests show unusual cytokine activity among those of low socioeconomic status as well as patients with post-traumatic stress and panic disorders.

It turns out that obese people have unusual cytokine readings, too, and these are often taken as the cause of weight-related illness. According to one theory, the presence of visceral fat cells can set off a biochemical chain reaction that leads to the inflammatory response. (Fat cells may even secrete the cytokines themselves.) As a result, someone who's fat and someone who's chronically stressed will be at risk for many of the same diseases.

It may be that obesity and stress are independent risk factors that happen to affect the body in similar ways. Or maybe chronic stress leads to weight gain, which in turn causes inflammation. According to epidemiologist Peter Muennig, there's another pathway from excess weight to disease. In his 2008 paper "The Body Politic: The Relationship Between Stigma and Obesity-Associated Disease," Muennig argues that the stress and shame of being fat causes those cytokine abnormalities. In other words, obesity makes you sick by stressing you out.

According to Muennig's theory, the health effects of obesity should vary with the intensity of anti-fat bias—the more abuse you take, the worse the disease. Women are more likely than men to have eating disorders, and they face greater weight-based discrimination in the overweight range. (According to Puhl, men get harsher treatment when they're really obese.) And, sure enough, women are seven times more likely to experience significant illness or death as a result of being overweight. (Obese women are especially vulnerable to clinical depression, which is itself a risk factor for cardiovascular disease.)

The Stigma of Obesity: Summary of Key Findings in Existing Weight Bias Research

	Strength of Evidence	
	Strong[c]	**Moderate**[b]
Employment Settings		
Obese employees perceive weight-based disparities in employment	X	
Obese employees experience a wage penalty (controlling for sociodemographic variables)	X	
Obese applicants face weight bias in job evaluations and hiring decisions	X	
Obese employees face disadvantaged employment outcomes due to weight bias		X
Health-Care Settings		
Health-care professionals endorse stereotypes and negative attitudes about obese patients	X	
Obese patients perceive biased treatment in health care		X
Interpersonal Relationships		
Obese individuals perceive weight bias from family members and friends		X
Media		
Overweight/obese characters are stigmatized in television and film	X	
Overweight/obese characters are stereotyped in children's media (TV, videos, cartoons)		X
Weight bias exists in news media		X
Psychological and Physical Health Consequences		
Weight bias increases vulnerability to depression, low self-esteem, and poor body image		X
Weight bias contributes to maladaptive eating behaviors among obese individuals	X	

[b]There is adequate evidence to suggest the phenomenon exists, but additional research is needed to strengthen current findings.
[c]Consistent evidence across a number of studies. Findings are clearly established.

TAKEN FROM: Adapted from Rebecca M. Puhl and Chelsea A. Heuer, "The Stigma of Obesity: A Review and Update," *Obesity*, vol. 17, November 5, 2009.

White people also appear to suffer disproportionately from weight-related illness, as compared with black people. According to Muennig, a black woman who's 5 feet 5 inches and less than 60 years old won't develop any weight-related risk of early death until she reaches 225 lbs. Meanwhile, a white woman of the same height and age group would hit the same threshold at 170 lbs. That fits with the idea that body-size norms differ among blacks and whites. (Black people also tend to be less susceptible to eating disorders and weight-based wage discrimination.)

There's plenty of evidence that body-shape discrimination plays a role in human disease outcomes.

There are some alternative explanations for these disparities. They might, for example, be an artifact of the crude way in which we measure obesity. Black people tend to have less abdominal fat (associated with cardiovascular disease) than white people given the same BMI reading, and women also tend to have more adipose tissue, and smaller waist-to-hip ratios, than men. But even the most accurate measures of fatness—like dual energy X-ray absorptiometry—don't really improve our ability to predict health outcomes across the population. It may be that the exact volume of adipose tissue in someone's body is less important than the way they look to others. (Muennig suggests that merely having "big bones" could be bad for your health.)

That's not to say obesity won't affect your body, independent of any social factors. As Muennig points out, obese lab rodents aren't likely to suffer much emotional abuse from their fellow mice, but they seem to have higher levels of pro-inflammatory cytokines nonetheless. Still, there's plenty of evidence that body-shape discrimination plays a role in human disease outcomes. Shortness, for example, is associated with an increased risk of coronary heart disease, diabetes, and early death—as well as lower wages and fewer long-term relationships. For some reason, though, the health effects of being short are worse for men than they are for women. Could it be that the social consequences of height and weight go in opposite directions?

If anti-fat bias can affect our bodies, then it's worth considering how an all-out war on obesity plays out in terms of public health. When we reach out to poor communities and educate them about the risks of being overweight, we are, in effect, exporting the weight stigma that happens to be most prevalent among rich, white people. Indeed, Rebecca Puhl says the reported prevalence of weight discrimination has increased by two-thirds (PDF) since the mid-1990s, while media coverage of the "obesity epidemic" has quintupled over roughly the same interval. (Meanwhile, the U.S. diet industry has just about doubled its annual revenues—to nearly $60 billion.)

A war on obesity would come at a significant cost to the fattest Americans.

We've worked hard to frame excess weight as a major health risk and a drain on the economy. The motivation is generous enough: Anti-obesity rhetoric encourages people to eat less and exercise more. But what if it also encourages discrimination? If that's the case, a war on obesity would come at a significant cost to the fattest Americans—in terms of lower wages, less education, and more stress-related illness.

Fat activists argue that the risks of such a policy far outweigh its potential benefits. (They say that doctors should encourage healthy lifestyles instead of trying to enforce an ideal body size.) But few mainstream public health advocates take such claims seriously. They point out that many interventions in poor communities focus on diet and exercise rather than weight per se. If BMI is used as a measure of success in these programs, that's because it's a quick way to see whether people really are pursuing a healthy lifestyle. For Kelly Brownell, director of the Rudd Center and a leading researcher on both health policy and weight bias, the dangers of discrimination are important but relatively modest. What about the idea that targeting obesity might be counterproductive for the fattest Americans? He doesn't buy it.

The fact is, very few researchers have tried to measure the combined health effects of anti-fat prejudice. Nor have legislators spent much effort on the social consequences of weight stigma. Only a handful of cities—Washington, D.C.; San Francisco, and Santa Cruz, Calif.—have passed laws to protect the rights of obese people, and there's only one state—Michigan—that forbids employers from discriminating on the basis of body size. If you're victimized for being fat anywhere else in the United States, good luck. You can sue your employer under the Americans with Disabilities Act, but you'll have to prove that your weight condition is something like being wheelchair bound or mentally retarded—not such a good way to reduce weight stigma overall.

Given the risks associated with weight stigma, we should at least reconsider our tendency to blame obesity for the country's health crisis. (I suggested last week that we could target poverty instead.) If obesity prevention measures do end up in the health bill, let's make sure they'll do more good than harm. The Rudd Center has called for a new federal ban on weight discrimination (PDF) or an expansion of the Civil Rights Act. Both would go a long way toward protecting the two-thirds of all Americans who are classified as overweight or obese.

Australians Face a Growing Rate of Genetic Discrimination

Kristine Barlow-Stewart

Kristine Barlow-Stewart is director of the Centre for Genetics Education at Royal North Shore Hospital in Sydney, Australia, and clinical associate professor of medicine at the University of Sydney. In the following viewpoint, she argues that genetic makeup should not be used to discriminate against individuals seeking life insurance policies or employment. In recent years, such discrimination has increased internationally and in Australia. She recommends that people who believe they have been discriminated against based on the results of genetic testing should seek legal advice to recoup their losses.

As you read, consider the following questions:

1. As described by the author, what was the nature of the policy developed by Australian life insurance companies in 2000?
2. What did the Genetic Discrimination Project (GDP) prove, according to the author?
3. What are three of the recommendations of the ALRC/ AHEC report?

Kristine Barlow-Stewart, "Genetic Discrimination: Australian Experiences and Policies," *GeneWatch*, vol. 22, no. 2, April-May 2009. Reprinted with the permission of *GeneWatch*, the magazine of the Council for Responsible Genetics.

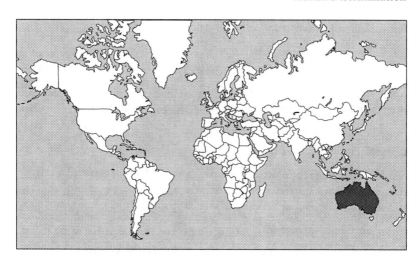

From the start of the Human Genome Project, and continuing in the post-mapping era, the ethical, legal and social issues associated with knowledge of a person's genetic information have been highlighted. In particular, there has been widespread international concern about the potential for differential treatment of healthy asymptomatic individuals based solely on their genetic makeup predicted from genetic testing or inferred from their family history. Most concern has been raised about this concept of "genetic discrimination" in commercial settings such as insurance and employment, unsurprising given the commercial value of predictive test information to such third parties.

In Australia in 2000, the announcement of findings of a study by [Australian researchers Kristine] Barlow-Stewart and [David] Keays that had identified 48 anonymously reported cases of genetic discrimination, in areas that included life insurance and employment, attracted significant media coverage. This was the impetus for the Australian Federal Government to request the Australian Law Reform Commission (ALRC) and the Australian Health Ethics Committee (AHEC) to conduct a comprehensive inquiry into the protection of human genetic information. The terms of reference governing the 2001–2003 inquiry were to recommend, in relation to human genetic information—and the samples from which the information is derived—how to best protect privacy interests, protect against *unfair* discrimination and ensure the highest ethical standards. The final report, *Essentially Yours[: The Protection of Human Genetic Information in Australia]* (2003) contained 144 recommendations directed at 31 bodies (government, regulators, educators, health professionals, insurers, employers and others) and covered the use of genetic information in a myriad of areas including risk-rated insurance, employment, identity testing and forensics and sport. Dr. Francis Collins declared the report "a truly phenomenal job . . . placing Australia ahead of what the rest of the world is doing." The Australian Government accepted the majority of the recommendations and implementation is proceeding; the National Health and Medical Research Council through its Human Genetics Advisory Committee was referred the areas of health, research and risk-rated insurance.

Genetic Information and Risk-Rated Insurance

In Australia, there is a national health system and private health insurance is not risk-rated. Therefore concerns regarding the potential for genetic discrimination are directed at the life insurance industry. The Disability Discrimination Act 1992 . . . acknowledges the commercial nature of life insurance as a form of voluntary mutually rated life insurance which of its nature involves differentiating between applicants on the basis of their health status and family histories of health problems. Therefore, life insurers in Australia are legally able to "discriminate" between people on the basis of their future health risks when making underwriting decision for life insurance products that include death cover, trauma and income protection, and long-term care insurance. Insurers are not in breach of the act if their actions are based on sound actuarial or other statistical data; thus the use of genetic information, whether obtained from genetic test results or reports of the health and causes of death of close family members, is not unfair discrimination under the act when used in this way. The recommendation of the ALRC/AHEC supported this concept that genetic information is no different to any other information for insurance purposes; that is, the general law on insurance contracts requires mutual disclosure in good faith of all relevant material and information that would help in risk assessment.

A cooperative approach, rather than a legislative one, has been taken in Australia in regard to genetic information and risk-rated insurance. The insurance industry has been very proactive in the use of genetic test results in underwriting by developing a policy, in 2000, that no insurer will require an applicant or insured person to have a DNA test. However, if a consumer has had a genetic test, or knows the results of relatives' genetic tests, they must declare them when applying for a new policy or changing an existing one. Once a policy is taken out and payments are maintained, it is described as "guaranteed renewable": no further information, such as the results of a genetic test, needs to be provided to the insurer. Nevertheless, the ALRC/AHEC report identified some issues that remained to be addressed to ensure that inappropriate use of genetic information does not occur within the industry. These include the continuing education of agents in the insurance industry to avoid inappropriate discriminatory use of the information; a clear understanding by customers of the mechanism to lodge complaints if it is felt that inappropriate decisions have been made; ensuring rigorous actuarial assessment of the applicability of a DNA test in the insurance setting; and existence of application and information sheets written in plain English so that applicants understand exactly what is required of them.

The need for these issues to be addressed has been underscored by data generated from the recently completed five-year Genetic Discrimination Project (GDP) which provides the first empirical evidence of the existence of genetic discrimination in the life insurance sector. The GDP also verified that some people do not undergo genetic testing that could be beneficial for their future health because they fear that the results could jeopardize their own or their relatives' access to life insurance. While the numbers of verified consumer-reported incidents were small, it is clear that a procedure needs to be set in place to ensure that genetic tests are used appropriately and underwriting is on the basis of actuarial data, requiring input from insurance industry bodies working with experts in genetics. The GDP could not have been completed without the support and cooperation of the Australian life insurance industry and it is hoped that further reforms will be generated on the continued basis of this cooperation.

Some people do not undergo genetic testing ... because they fear that the result could jeopardize their own ... access to life insurance.

It will also be essential for insurers to address the potential impact of their requirements for full disclosure of genetic test information on the recruitment of volunteers in genetics research projects. The consent process needs to make it clear that if their test results will be provided to volunteers as part of their involvement in the research, they will have to declare the results in their insurance application or when changing their insurance policy, despite potential adverse effects. It is also important to note that research participants who are not given test results are under no obligation to disclose their involvement in the research project.

Genetic Information and Employment

The ALRC/AHEC recommendations, accepted by the government, covered the use of genetic information in employment-based health screening, health surveillance and other health assessments, including those for occupational health and safety. Given that there is no linkage between employment and health insurance in Australia, the issue is the balance between the interests of employers, employees and the public and the inappropriate use of genetic information in the workplace. In the occupational health and safety setting, there is the potential to use genetic information to identify persons who are susceptible to workplace hazards, or who pose a risk to themselves or others as a result of possible future onset of a genetic disease and to monitor employees' health over time where there is industrial exposure to, for example, toxic chemicals or radiation. However, concern has also been expressed about other drivers for its use, including economic factors to limit payouts in the case of workplace injury and liability. In one of the cases verified by the GDP, in a workers' compensation claim of a woman who had injured her back at work, the tribunal adjudicating the case requested that her claim be subject to having a predictive genetic test to prove that she had not inherited the faulty gene for Huntington's disease, of which she had a family history. This was based on the erroneous view that her fall may have been due to the first signs of the condition, and so was an inappropriate and discriminatory request, denying her the right to make an autonomous choice whether to know her genetic makeup in regard to this late onset and untreatable neurological condition.

Despite this case, the GDP study found that there is currently no evidence of systematic use of genetic testing or other genetic information by Australian employers for screening or monitoring purposes, confirming the conclusions of the ALRC/AHEC report. Although there was little evidence of Australian employers *currently* using genetic information, it was seen as almost inevitable that, as tests become cheaper and more reliable, employers would seek to make use of such information in the future. The GDP study also confirmed this view, with a number of employers expressing interest in the future use of genetic tests if they became more reliable.

In contrast to policies directed towards the insurance industry, the ALRC/AHEC recommendations advocated changes to legislation that would amount to a general prohibition of the use of genetic information by employers, with very limited exceptions primarily on occupational health and safety grounds. In the exceptions in which a genetic test may be used in the employment setting, there needs to be strong evidence of a clear connection between the working environment and the development of the condition; it must be shown that the condition may seriously endanger the health or safety of the employee; and the test must be a scientifically reliable method of screening for the condition. Moreover, policies would need to be developed governing how the DNA sample is stored and protected against being used for other purposes or the destruction of DNA samples when an employee leaves the organisation.

Again, the Australian Federal Government endorsed the broad thrust of these recommendations, but they have yet to be legislatively implemented.

Only a relatively small number of cases of genetic discrimination have been taken to tribunals seeking legal redress.

Seeking Redress for Genetic Discrimination

From the GDP's analysis of cases that came before antidiscrimination tribunals and other relevant bodies in Australia, it is clear that only a relatively small number of cases of genetic discrimination have been taken to tribunals seeking legal redress. This view was confirmed by consumers who reported financial and emotional barriers to seeking redress, as well as not knowing where or how to complain. It is essential therefore to promote and facilitate avenues of complaint and redress when policies or legislation are implemented in order to prevent or limit genetic discrimination.

The empirical evidence of genetic discrimination provided by the work of the GDP has finally put to rest the perception that the phenomenon is a measure of "genetic dread" in society—that it simply reflected community-based fear rather than reality. Life insurance was the main context within which genetic discrimination occurred in the Australian investigation, but this does not discount the possibility of genetic discrimination in health or other risk-rated insurance in other countries. The response made by each country to prevent or minimize the harm associated with the broadening applications of genetic technologies will necessarily be balanced by the economic, legal and ethical concerns within different political systems. What is undeniable, however, is that such policies and/or legislation must be put into place to maximize the benefits to society generated by developments in this dynamic field of genetic science and medicine.

India Still Discriminates Against Lepers Even After a Cure Has Been Found

Ramesh Menon

Ramesh Menon is a best-selling Indian author and documentary filmmaker. In the following viewpoint, he argues that discrimination against lepers remains a challenge in India. Although a cure for the disease was discovered in 1982, people still fear catching the disease from infected and formerly infected persons. Menon reports on recent campaigns by world organizations to educate the public about leprosy, and he confirms that until attitudes about the disease and those who suffer from it change, eradicating the disease will be that much more difficult.

As you read, consider the following questions:

1. Around what percentage of the human population is naturally immune to leprosy?
2. At one time, 10 percent of leprosy patients suffered from deformity because the disease was detected too late. To what percentage has that declined?
3. What percentage of leprosy patients live in India?

When Mahatma Gandhi was once called to inaugurate a leprosy home, he said: "I regret I cannot come to open a leprosy home, but I shall be very happy if you invite me to

Ramesh Menon, "Leprosy Nearly Eliminated, Challenges Remain," India Together, August 28, 2006. Reprinted by permission.

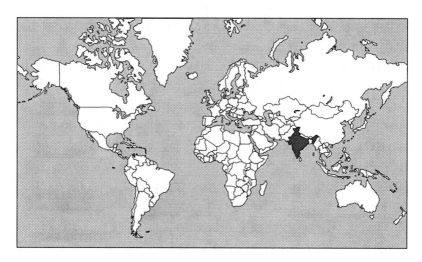

close it." That was around 65 years ago. Leprosy was seen as a major curse. Patients then had no access to medicine and were social outcasts living on the fringes of society or begging for a living.

An Ancient Disease

Leprosy is one of the ancient diseases known to humankind. It existed practically in every continent at one time, leaving behind terrifying images of mutilation, rejection and exclusion from society. Ancient Indian classical texts dating back to the sixth century refer to it.

Over 95 per cent of us are naturally immune to leprosy. That is why it is easy to control and treat as only less than 10 per cent of the cases are infectious. The disease spreads only through prolonged contact with infected persons who have not been treated.

Till the seventies, the only drug available to treat leprosy was Dapsone. It took long to cure and had to be consumed for years. But, in 1982, the WHO [World Health Organization] whipped up a cocktail of three drugs that worked as a miracle destroying 99.2 per cent of the leprosy bacilli with the first dose. Most patients get cured within two months now.

What was done was mixing Dapsone with drug formulations of Rifampicin and Clofazimine. This miracle drug was called Multidrug Therapy (MDT). It was made available freely through primary health centers. In the early eighties, there were as many as 15 million suffering from leprosy all over the world. Today, the figure is less than 500,000. The number of new cases is decreasing every day. "We have a great opportunity to control leprosy spreading with MDT," says S.K. Noordeen, former medical director of the WHO leprosy elimination programme, in Geneva.

Today, there has been a dramatic change. India, which was one of the worst countries affected, detected only around 161,000 new cases last year [2005] and the cases under treatment this year is only about 98,000. This still looks like a huge figure in comparison to other countries, but that is because of India's huge population and even one case in 10,000 works out to be a huge figure. In June the benchmark figure had come down to 0.86 cases per 10,000.

The number of new cases is decreasing every day.

Dramatic Change

The profile of leprosy has also changed. Earlier, 10 per cent of the patients suffered from deformity as the disease was detected late. Now, it is down to two per cent and should come down even more. Even leprosy colonies have changed. Normal people also live among them now as the fear of the disease has lessened as medicines can cure.

Dr Derek Lobo, regional advisor for leprosy and other diseases targeted for elimination and eradication of the World Health Organization at New Delhi, is optimistic that by the end of 2007, all the six Indian states and the two union territories will have achieved the 'elimination' status. The World Health Organization is presently aiming at ensuring that all countries get to the elimination stage first. It is presently not even talking of total eradication, as it would take decades. In India, the states that still have more than one case per 10,000 populations are Bihar, Uttar Pradesh, Jharkhand, Chhattisgarh, West Bengal and Delhi. Two union territories that are lagging behind are Chandigarh and Dadra/Nagar Haveli. But on the whole, India has eliminated it as a public health problem.

There is enough evidence to be optimistic. Andhra Pradesh and Tamilnadu were two of the southern states where prevalence of the disease was high. Today, it is well under control with medicines easily available in all primary health centers. There is also an increased awareness of how it can be cured and a political will to fight it. About 15 years ago, Tamilnadu had one lakh leprosy cases. Today, it is negligible. The state used 2500 personnel solely to trigger off a sustained campaign. Then, it motivated its 6000 odd workers to work towards elimination.

Very recently, Orissa has achieved the elimination goal, and Chief Minister Naveen Patnaik is scheduled to formally announce the same in a state-level health workshop in September [2006], after current verification of figures is complete.

Says Yohei Sasakawa, chairman of the Nippon Foundation, Japan, and the WHO goodwill ambassador for the elimination of leprosy, who gave 10 million dollars to fund medicine for leprosy patients: "India has achieved a great milestone. The challenge now is to work at all levels and ensure a commitment made at all levels of the hierarchy to banish leprosy. Every family in India should be informed about leprosy; about it being a totally curable disease; that drugs are available free; that there is absolutely no cause to fear the disease, and there is no reason for discrimination." In the last four years, Sasakawa has been to India 19 times to network with organisations and government bodies that are fighting leprosy. "In the last 26 years, since the development of Multidrug Therapy

(MDT) to cure leprosy, 11 million Indians have been cured, but people continue to treat them as if they still have the disease and could transmit it to them," he said.

Sasakawa has been involved in leprosy elimination for more than 30 years. His efforts have earned him worldwide praise and awards, including the Millennium Gandhi Award. Additionally, in 2001, WHO named him special ambassador for the elimination of leprosy, a title that he has worked hard to give meaning to. Most recently, he has become WHO's goodwill ambassador for leprosy elimination.

Challenges Remain

Yet, the fact remains that India is still the home to nearly 60 per cent of the world's leprosy patients.

Leprosy is not fatal but those who contract it are feared. So they get isolated and are condemned to spend the rest of their life in a sickening whirlpool of discrimination. Ironically, this is in spite of the fact that today leprosy is completely curable within 6 to 12 months with MDT. Prompt treatment ensures that there is no deformity. The drug has cured over 14 million worldwide. There were 122 endemic countries that had the disease. Today, only nine remain. One of them is India.

Former health minister, Karan Singh, of the [National] Congress Party, says that he is delighted to see the number of cases go down drastically, but says that India must work at total eradication even if it will take a long time and lots of committed work. Only total elimination in India will mitigate stigma, he said.

Karan Singh says one idea worth exploring is to get religious leaders to talk about the fact that it is not a genetic disease and it can easily be cured. They could also be used to spread the word that it is not God's curse and is just a medical problem, he added.

Sharatchandra Damodar Gokhale, chairman of the International Leprosy Union, says that the need of the hour is to give leprosy a human face. In August 2005, the UN [United Nations] Sub-Commission on the Promotion and Protection of Human Rights passed a resolution calling on governments to prohibit discrimination against leprosy patients, recovered persons and their families.

Leprosy is not fatal but those who contract it are feared.

Gokhale says that the strategy to fight leprosy has to be culture specific with a clear understanding of the community one is dealing with. Only then can one fight the cynicism about the disease and the myths that go with it. Awareness is the key. Residents of Rajnandgaon district in Madhya Pradesh see leprosy as an ailment that can easily be treated. This is because Danida, a Danish organisation, drove out fear of the disease with a systematic awareness campaign.

Seeking Societal Acceptance

Gokhale says that the biggest challenge is to get society to accept the cured leprosy patients. Most of them painfully discovered that even their families did not want them as the stigma was so strong. "Leprosy may be eliminated as a public health problem in India as in most states it is only one case per ten thousand. But what about rehabilitating the thousands of cured patients who linger on the sidelines of society as no one wants to even touch them. Many of them are beggars in urban India as it is the only way to get a meal. They are not given jobs as they are disfigured and there is tremendous fear of the disease."

Gokhale recounts of an instance where an aged inmate of a home set up for cured leprosy patients begged him not to introduce her to a bureaucrat who was to be the chief guest at that home that day. Gokhale agreed. After the bureaucrat left,

What Is Leprosy?

Leprosy is caused by *Mycobacterium leprae,* a slender rod-shaped bacillus discovered by [Gerhard] Hansen in 1873.

The disease mainly affects the skin, peripheral nerves, and mucosa of the upper respiratory tract, eyes, and also some internal organs such as bones and testes. Affected patients feel a loss of sensation on parts of their body that have some skin eruptions or pigmentation.

As the bacilli affects the nerves, patients lose sensation in their hands, feet, and eyes. This often ends up in disfigurement as sores caused by injuries get ignored, as it does not hurt.

Ramesh Menon,
"Leprosy Nearly Eliminated, Challenges Remain,"
India Together, August 26, 2006. www.indiatogether.org.

he asked her why she had made the strange request. She said that her husband and in-laws had told him that his mother was dead when she contracted leprosy and was removed from home. "I want him to continue living without the burden of knowing that I was alive in a leprosy home," she said tearfully.

Most of them painfully discovered that even their families did not want them as the stigma was so strong.

The global appeal against leprosy stigma released by Sasakawa early this year underlined that 20 million cured leprosy affected people in the world today live a life "better than death, but worse than living" for no fault of their own. Besides, around 100 million family members also suffer from stigma and discrimination even though the victims today are fully cured. They live on the fringes of society, unwanted, uncared for and discriminated against. They do not feel they have any human rights as it is denied to them.

Removing stigma is going to be no easy task. Almost three thousand years of history, culture, myths and wrong perceptions have shaped the public beliefs regarding leprosy:

- It is dangerous and unclean.

- It is God's curse and his way to punish with hideous deformities to their faces and limbs.

- It is not just the affliction of the body, but of the soul as it embodies an immoral life.

- It is incurable and spreads by touch.

Almost three thousand years of history, culture, myths and wrong perceptions have shaped the public beliefs regarding leprosy.

The truth is that all of these are untrue and scientifically proven to be false.

Unfortunately, except for the last quarter of a century, it was untreatable. Those affected were forced to live and die an undignified life. The affected parts had no physical pain, but their lives were punctuated with pain all through. The stigma that stuck to them was worse than seeing body parts like the tip of the nose, fingers and toes just disappear.

Towards Victory at the Last Mile

The International Leprosy Union has started a programme called Lokdoot, in which those cured from leprosy fan into society and openly say that they had the disease and had got completely cured. Bharat Scouts and Guides work with the Lokdoots, taking them and their message to the community.

Today, there is a two-pronged attempt to fight the stigma and ensure welfare of the people affected by leprosy. One, the

National Forum [for Leprosy Affected People in India], under the leadership of Dr P.K. Gopal, who has been cured, is organising workshops to train the leaders of the affected people of some 700 leprosy colonies of India in articulating and solving their colony-specific problems and know their rights and duties. Secondly, a trust with an initial endowment of 10 million US dollars is being set up by Sasakawa in India, with a matching grant of 10 million more from India Inc and organizations here, to go into vocational training of the women and children of the people affected by leprosy and their general welfare measures. The trust is likely to be operational in a few months.

Leprosy workers are convinced that the key to helping the cured is to ensure their economic independence.

However, all these will bear fruit only when people dispel the myths of curse and infection associated with leprosy and learn to accept the scientific truths that the disease is completely curable with MDT in less than a year, deformity is not the disease but the consequence of it which can be fully avoided if treated in time, and that the society will continue doing a grave injustice to the affected people if their human rights to life, liberty, job, property and free movement are curtailed and even denied.

Leprosy workers are convinced that the key to helping the cured is to ensure their economic independence. Wherever they have gotten jobs and are able to stand on their feet, they have earned respect. The Jal Mehta Rehabilitation Centre in Pune, for instance, has now a factory where parts of Telco trucks are manufactured by those cured from leprosy. It has helped many of them see a new day. The road ahead for complete eradication of leprosy from India is not as easy as it looks, but a concentrated campaign and strategy will help it slowly inch towards that dream.

Periodical and Internet Sources Bibliography

The following articles have been selected to supplement the diverse views presented in this chapter.

Jeanne Hayes	"Female Infertility in the Workplace: Understanding the Scope of the Pregnancy Discrimination Act," *Connecticut Law Review*, vol. 42, no. 4, May 2010.
Helen Henderson	"Discrimination, Disrespect a Fact for People Living with Disabilities, Study Finds," *Toronto Star*, May 29, 2010.
National Conference of State Legislatures	"Genetics and Health Insurance State Anti-Discrimination Laws," January 2008. www.ncsl.org.
National Human Genome Research Institute	"Genetic Discrimination in Health Insurance or Employment," November 3, 2010. www.genome.gov.
New Scientist	"Does Not Hiring Smokers Improve Health or Damage It?," vol. 201, no. 2693, January 28, 2009.
People's Daily Online	"Hepatitis Carriers Fight Job Discrimination in SW China City," September 18, 2009. http://english.peopledaily.com.cn.
Suzannah Phillips	"Forced Sterilization and Discrimination in Chile," *Akimbo* (blog), October 27, 2010. http://blog.iwhc.org.
Eleanor Smeal	"A Title IX for Health Care?," *Ms.*, vol. 20, no. 2, Spring 2010.
Sondra Solovay and Esther Rothblum	"No Fear of Fat," *Chronicle of Higher Education*, November 8, 2009.
Karen Wright	"New Law Bans Genetic Discrimination," *Discover*, vol. 30, no. 1, January 2009.

GLOBALVIEWPOINTS

CHAPTER 2

Gender and Sexuality Discrimination

Hong Kong Should Enact Antidiscrimination Laws to Protect Gays, Lesbians, and Bisexuals

Phil C. W. Chan

Phil C. W. Chan is a legal scholar specializing in human rights, international law, and constitutional law. In the following viewpoint, he argues that Hong Kong's lack of antidiscrimination laws is harmful to gays, lesbians, and bisexuals. He traces the history of the current attitudes toward Hong Kong's largest minority group to demonstrate the need to overhaul antiquated attitudes about sexuality. Chan also asserts that the international community needs a set of such laws as well. Protecting sexual minorities is as important as protecting other minorities, according to Chan.

As you read, consider the following questions:

1. What accomplishments does the author attribute to the 1945 San Francisco Conference?

2. According to the author, what percentages of the population of Hong Kong were prejudiced against sexual minorities in 2000?

Phil C.W. Chan, "The Lack of Sexual Orientation Anti-Discrimination Legislation in Hong Kong: Breach of International and Domestic Legal Obligations," *International Journal of Human Rights*, vol. 9, no. 1, Spring 2005, pp. 69–71, 94–95; notes 96-97, 106. Reprinted by permission of the publisher Taylor & Francis, Ltd., http://www.informaworld.com.

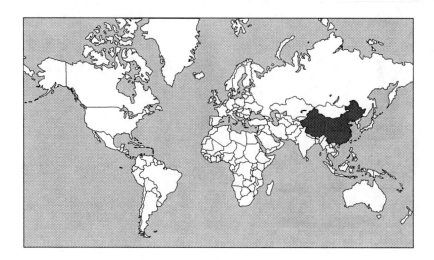

3. Which two episodes changed the course of the legal battle for sexual minorities in Hong Kong, as stated by the author?

When statesmen in the 1945 San Francisco Conference realised the appalling atrocities that international indifference to domestic human rights abuse had caused, they started to foster international human rights law and established the United Nations.[2] In the meantime, however, they failed to address the sufferings that innumerable gays, lesbians, and bisexuals had endured in concentration camps,[3] and persecution against sexual minorities has persisted.[4] The proclamation of the Universal Declaration of Human Rights (UDHR),[5] the International Covenant on Civil and Political Rights (ICCPR),[6] and the International Covenant on Economic, Social and Cultural Rights (ICESCR)[7] did not address the injustice since these instruments did not expressly include sexual orientation as a prohibited ground of discrimination. There are also no international instruments (except the Charter of Fundamental Rights of the European Union[8] which, by definition, binds only the 25 Members States of the European Union) that expressly prohibit discrimination on grounds of sexual orientation, whereas sex,[9] race,[10] and religion[11] are covered. Morgan and Walker lament the international community as '. . . complicitously silent regarding the abuses suffered worldwide by gay men and lesbians'.[12] Nonetheless, thanks to the perseverance of civil rights lobbyists;[13] to recognition of the need for legal reform at both international and domestic levels; and to the progressiveness of international organs and domestic courts in interpreting existing human rights instruments and constitutions as prohibiting sexual orientation discrimination, the principle of equality as forcefully stated by Tony Blair has finally begun to truly develop.

This positive remark, however, cannot conceal the brutal reality that there are still many countries that remain static, ambivalent or even hostile to suggestions for legal reform *vis-à-vis* sexual orientation. Though an international metropolis entrenched with a dynamic population, Hong Kong is unfortunately on the list. In 2000, the Hong Kong Polytechnic University and Caritas jointly conducted a survey which indicated that 54.6 per cent of the population carried prejudices against sexual minorities.[14] A plausible explanation naturally was the lack of sexual orientation anti-discrimination legislation in Hong Kong. The importance of such legislation, as Chapman puts it, is that

> adjudication provides a forum through which the stories of gay men and lesbians may themselves enter public discourse and challenge commonly held views and assumptions about gay men and lesbians. A successful public hearing of a complaint sends a message, not only to gay men and lesbians, but to the wider community as well, that gay and lesbian oppression exists and is challengeable.[15]

Of course, such legislation will, more importantly, also provide redress to individuals who endure sexual orientation discrimination or harassment as it occurs. This article, accordingly, seeks to outline the distinctive legal developments concerning homosexuality in Hong Kong and to critique the

LGTBI Rights in the World (by Country or Region)

Persecution—death penalty or imprisonment for same-sex acts:

Death penalty

Nigeria, Iran, Mauritania, Saudi Arabia, Sudan, United Arab Emirates, Yemen

Imprisonment, no precise indication of the length

Angola, Djibouti, Lesotho, Namibia, Sao Tome & Principe, Swaziland

Imprisonment from 1 month to 10 years

Afghanistan, Algeria, Bahrain, Belize, Benin, Bhutan, Botswana, Brunei, Burkina Faso, Cameroon, Cook Islands, Democratic Republic of Congo, Dominica, Egypt, Equatorial Guinea, Eritrea, Ethiopia, Gaza, Ghana, Grenada, Guinea, Guinea-Bissau, Jamaica, Kuwait, Lebanon, Liberia, Libya, Maldives, Mauritios, Morocco, Myanmar/Burma, Nepal, Niger, Oman, Palau, Panama, Qatar, Saint Lucia, Saint Kitts and Nevis, Saint Vincent and the Grenadines, Samoa, Senegal, Somalia, Sri Lanka, Syria, Togo, Tonga, Tunisia, Turkmenistan, Uzbekistan, Zimbabwe

Imprisonment from 11 years to a life-long sentence

Antigua and Barbuda, Bangladesh, Barbados, Guyana, India, Kenya, Kiribati, Malawi, Malaysia, Nauru, Pakistan, Papua New Guinea, Seychelles, Sierra Leone, Singapore, Solomon Islands, Tanzania, Trinidad and Tobago, Turkish Republic of North Cyprus, Tuvalu, Uganda, Zambia

continued

lack of a Sexual Orientation Discrimination Ordinance in this former British colony. Legal implications, both international and domestic, arising from such lack of anti-discrimination legislation will then be assessed. Given the recent developments on this subject through the establishment by the Legislature's Home Affairs Panel in 2000 of a Subcommittee to Study Discrimination on the Ground of Sexual Orientation (hereafter Subcommittee) aimed at exploring sexual orientation discrimination in specific areas[16] and ultimately reporting its work to the Panel,[17] it is hoped that this analysis will be able to contribute to enactment of a piece of legislation that propounds equality among all.

LGTBI Rights in the World [CONTINUED]

Recognition—countries which recognise same-sex unions and introduced registration systems:

Marriage

Belgium, Canada, Netherlands, South Africa, Spain

Equal (almost equal) substitute for marriage

Tasmania, New Zealand, Australian Capital Territory, Greenland, Iceland, Luxembourg, Norway, Sweden, Finland, Denmark, Germany, United Kingdom, Switzerland

Clearly inferior substitute for marriage

Andorra, Czech Republic, France, French Guyana, Slovenia, Uruguay

Protection—countries which introduced laws prohibiting discrimination on the grounds of sexual orientation (in some countries such bans included in national constitutions and in some countries in other laws: areas of protections from discrimination varies):

Australia, Austria, Bosnia Herzegovina, Bulgaria, Colombia, Costa Rica, Croatia, Cyprus, Ecuador, Estonia, Fiji, Georgia, Greece, Hungary, Ireland, Israel, Italy, Kosovo, Latvia, Lithuania, Malta, Mexico, Mozambique, Poland, Portugal, Romania, Serbia, Slovakia, Tawain, Venezuela

TAKEN FROM: ReligiousTolerance.org, "LGTBI Rights in the World," 2008.

Legal Developments Concerning Homosexuality in Hong Kong

Upon the end of the Opium War between Imperial Qing China and Great Britain, in 1842 the Treaty of Nanking was signed which ceded Hong Kong to the British Empire.[18] English law was then imported into the then colony and the complete ban on homosexuality that had its origin in Henry VIII's Buggery Act[19] was no exception.[20]

Eventually, however, sentiment against state interference mounted in England after certain prominent figures were prosecuted for gay-related sexual offences.[21] Consequently, the

Wolfenden committee was established in 1954 to investigate the role of criminal law in the private domain of homosexuality. The committee concluded its investigation in 1957 and its findings[22] fervently stated that '. . . there must remain a realm of private morality and immorality which is, in brief and crude terms, not the law's business'.[23] Though with considerable delay, Parliament in Westminster eventually decriminalised homosexuality in 1967.[24] Although other Commonwealth Members, Crown Colonies and British Crown Dependencies generally followed suit,[25] Hong Kong did not reflect or follow this trend.[26]

Two episodes changed the course of legal developments in Hong Kong on the subject of homosexuality, however. In the late 1970s, a Special Investigation Unit was established in Hong Kong for the arrest of gays, lesbians, and bisexuals, especially those who were law enforcement officers (including lawyers). This incident, known as Operation Rockcorry, led 424 individuals to petition the Government for the decriminalisation of homosexuality. Then, on 15 January 1980, in an operation endeavouring to arrest a fellow police inspector named John MacLennan who was allegedly a bisexual suspected of eight counts of gross indecency (namely, a crime involving conduct of a sexual nature, short of anal intercourse and perhaps necessitating no physical contact,[27] between two or more men), the police found him mysteriously dead. It was then alleged that MacLennan had been murdered for possessing information on high-ranked government officials who were gay. Press coverage was extensive in both Hong Kong and Scotland from which MacLennan originated. An inquiry was subsequently conducted which concluded that the cause of MacLennan's death was suicide.[28] In response to these two episodes, the Law Reform Commission was set up in 1980. The commission published its findings[29] three years later, declaring that '. . . it should not be a function of the law to enforce moral judgments in areas where there is no need to protect others . . .'[30] Regrettably, the administration did not act on this vocal statement due to societal prejudices against homosexuality.[31]

Despite the lifting of the outright ban on homosexuality, certain but definite inequities have remained.

It was, quite ironically, the tragic Tiananmen massacre of 1989[32] that changed the whole course of events. Confidence in the Hong Kong Government and in the future of Hong Kong sank 'to an all-time low',[33] and fear of the imminent transfer of sovereignty[34] and potential human rights violations in Hong Kong reawakened. To allay public concern, the Hong Kong Legislature assessed the viability of a Bill of Rights modelled on the ICCPR (which itself is incorporated into the Basic Law, i.e., the mini-Constitution of Hong Kong as of 1 July 1997)[35] and ultimately enacted the Hong Kong Bill of Rights Ordinance in July 1991. This Bill of Rights was a watershed in the gay rights movement in Hong Kong. It provides, *inter alia*, that '[n]o one shall be subjected to arbitrary or unlawful interference with his privacy, home or correspondence, nor to unlawful attacks on his honour and reputation. Everyone has the right to the protection of the law against such interference or attacks'.[36] The administration then put forward a Crimes (Amendment) Bill aimed at decriminalisation of consensual sexual activity between male adults[37] as it acknowledged that '[i]t hardly needs saying that the laws of Hong Kong are required, in accordance with our international obligations, to be consistent with those obligations'.[38] After a heated legislative debate,[39] the Crimes (Amendment) Bill was passed in July 1991 (after the enactment of the Bill of Rights Ordinance);[40] consensual sexual activity between male persons is now regulated by s.118C of the Crimes Ordinance which provides that '[a] man who commits buggery [i.e., anal intercourse] with a man under the age of 21; or being under the age of 21 commits buggery with another man . . . shall be liable . . . to imprisonment for life'.[41] Such 'tolerance', however, is subject to a perplexing requirement of 'in private'.[42] Despite the lifting of the outright ban on homosexuality, certain but definite inequities have remained, details of which the present Author has elucidated in another forum.[43]. . .

Conclusion

Gays, lesbians, and bisexuals arguably constitute the largest minority group in Hong Kong.[294] Nonetheless, they also form the most discriminated against minority group in this East-meets-West city[295] and endure discrimination and harassment whilst without protection of the law. Despite calls from local and international civil rights lobbyists and international legal organs for more vigorous legal reform on sexual orientation, the Hong Kong government has persistently refused to enact sexual orientation anti-discrimination legislation which, if enacted, will certainly contribute to reducing, if not eliminating outright, inequality arising from sexual orientation hostilities and prejudices. As Wintemute forcefully points out, '[a]nti-discrimination protection . . . has in most jurisdictions been the single most important step in reducing lesbian and gay inequality. . .'[296]

The international community . . . must also take such initiatives as to establish international legal rules and principles.

The Home Affairs Panel's establishment of a Subcommittee to Study Discrimination on the Ground of Sexual Orientation was a laudable move that could have the effect of publicly (though little media coverage has been given to Subcommittee discussions) and officially acknowledging the daily sufferings and suppression endured by sexual minorities.

More importantly, the Subcommittee has the ability to discuss the viability and significance of sexual orientation anti-discrimination legislation and potentially also to propose such legislation to the Legislature.[297] On the other hand, it must be emphasised that the Subcommittee must itself be impartial and objective in understanding and critiquing views opposing sexual orientation anti-discrimination legislation whilst bearing in mind the harmful effects of discrimination and harassment upon sexual minorities. As Chief Justice Dickson maintained in Oakes,[298] a Supreme Court of Canada case concerning the presumption of innocence:

> The court must be guided by the values and principles essential to a free and democratic society which I believe embody, to name but a few, respect for the inherent dignity of the human person, commitment to social justice and equality, accommodation of a wide variety of beliefs, respect for cultural and group identity, and faith in social and political institutions which enhance the participation of individuals and groups in a society.[299]

Petersen opines that '[a]s a relative newcomer to the field of anti-discrimination law, Hong Kong [is] in a position to learn from the experience of other jurisdictions and adopt a progressive model'.[300] It is imperative that the Subcommittee not manipulate itself or be manipulated as a mere political tool or masquerade, and it is hoped that this analysis could add to the Subcommittee's undertaking, in addition to disseminating and analysing information on this important issue to the local and the international communities.

In addition to affirming that national and municipal protection for sexual minorities against discrimination and harassment be indispensable, the international community, bearing in mind the appalling persecution during the Second World War against minorities, which included sexual minorities, and the eminent principle of equality for and among all as enshrined in the UDHR,[301] must also take such initiatives as to establish international legal rules and principles *vis-à-vis* sexual orientation anti-discrimination. As Reuther emphasises, '[t]he international human rights community must acknowledge the plight of gay and lesbian people around the world and pledge to protect them from abuse before the full scope of queer persecution can be known and understood'.[302] International instruments, in the form of a multilateral treaty such as the Convention on the Elimination of All Forms of Discrimination Against Women or at least of a United Nations General Assembly declaration, are highly desirable and ought to be proclaimed without delay.

Notes

2. See Charter of the United Nations, signed at the conclusion of the United Nations Conference on International Organisation held in San Francisco on 26 June 1945; entry into force: 24 October 1945.

3. For an account of Hitler's purge against sexual minorities, see Richard Plant, *The Pink Triangle: The Nazi War Against Homosexuals* (New York: H. Holt, 1986).

4. For a comprehensive account of the persecution sexual minorities have faced since the Second World War, see Nicole LaViolette and Sandra Whitworth, 'No Safe Haven: Sexuality as a Universal Human Right and Gay and Lesbian Activism in International Politics', *Millennium: Journal of International Studies*, Vol.23 (1994), p.563.

5. Adopted and proclaimed by United Nations General Assembly Resolution 217A(III) of 10 December 1948.

6. Adopted and opened for signature, ratification and accession by United Nations General Assembly Resolution 2200A(XXI) of 16 December 1966; entry into force: 23 March 1976.

7. Adopted and opened for signature, ratification and accession by United Nations General Assembly Resolution 2200A(XXI) of 16 December 1966; entry into force: 3 January 1976.

8. Signed and proclaimed by Presidents of the European Parliament, of the Council of the European Union, and of the European Commission at the European Council meeting in Nice on 7 December 2000. Art.21 of the Charter states that '[a]ny discrimination based on any ground such as sex, race, colour, ethnic or social origin, genetic features, language, religion or belief, political or any other opinion, membership of a national minority, property, birth, disability, age or sexual orientation shall be prohibited.'

9. E.g., Convention on the Elimination of All Forms of Discrimination Against Women, adopted and opened for signature, ratification and accession by United Nations General Assembly Resolution 34/180 of 18 December 1979; entry into force: 3 September 1981; Declaration on the Elimination of All Forms of Discrimination Against Women, proclaimed by United Nations General Assembly Resolution 2263(XXII) of 7 November 1967.

10. E.g., International Convention on the Elimination of All Forms of Racial Discrimination, adopted and opened for signature and ratification by United Nations General Assembly Resolution 2106(XX) of 21 December 1965; entry into force: 4 January 1969; United Nations Declaration on the Elimination of All Forms of Racial Discrimination, proclaimed by United Nations General Assembly Resolution 1904 (XVIII) of 20 November 1963; Declaration on Race and Racial Prejudice, adopted and proclaimed by the General Conference of the United Nations Educational, Scientific and Cultural Organization at its 20th Session on 27 November 1978.

11. E.g., Declaration on the Elimination of All Forms of Intolerance and of Discrimination Based on Religion or Belief, proclaimed by United Nations General Assembly Resolution 36/55 of 25 November 1981.

12. Wayne Morgan and Kristen Walker, 'Tolerance and Homosex: A Policy of Control and Containment', *Melbourne University Law Review*, Vol.20 (1995), p.202 at p.206.

13. Amnesty International officially and explicitly affirmed in 1979 that persons imprisoned for advocating sexual orientation rights be included as prisoners of conscience; such inclusion was expanded in 1991 to those imprisoned solely for their sexual minority identity, whether real or presumed, and for their private practice of consensual same-sex sexual activities; see Amnesty International, *Breaking the Silence: Human Rights Violations Based on Sexual Orientation* (London: Author, 1997), p.63.

14. The findings of the survey were published in *Apple Daily*, a local Chinese newspaper, at A6 (27 November 2000): 'Homosexuals and Prostitutes Most Discriminated Against'.

15. Anna Chapman, 'Sexuality and Workplace Oppression', *Melbourne University Law Review*, Vol.20 (1995), p.311 at p.342. The author, for a detailed analysis of how law intervenes in the evolution of cultural perceptions, cites, at fn.155, Wayne Morgan, 'Identifying Evil for What It Is: Tasmania, Sexual Perversity and the United Nations', *Melbourne University Law Review*, Vol.19 (1994), p.740.

16. Subcommittee to Study Discrimination on the Ground of Sexual Orientation, 'Minutes of Meeting of the Subcommittee to Study Discrimination on the Ground of Sexual Orientation held on 10 January 2001': LC Paper No.CB(2)790/00–01, para.4.

17. Ibid., para.3.

18. Treaty of Nanking of 1842, in Clive Parry (ed.), *The Consolidated Treaty Series*, Vol.93, p.465; reproduced in Andrew Byrnes and Johannes Chan (eds.), *Public Law and Human Rights: A Hong Kong Sourcebook* (Hong Kong: Butterworths, 1993), pp.5–7.

19. 25 Henr. VIII c.6. According to H. Montgomery Hyde, *The Other Love: An Historical and Contemporary Survey of Homosexuality in Britain* (London: Heinemann, 1970), p.40, the statute was repealed in 1553, by 1 Mar. c.1; but reinstated intact in 1563, by 5 Eliz. I c.17. Mandatory death penalty was replaced by life imprisonment under s.61 of the Offences Against the Person Act 1861 as maximum penalty for the offence of homosexual buggery.

20. Offences Against the Person Ordinance 1865, s.50.

21. See Donald West and Richard Green (eds.), *Sociolegal Control of Homosexuality: A Multi-Nation Comparison* (New York: Plenum Press, 1997), p.198.

22. Great Britain Committee on Homosexual Offences and Prostitution, *Report of the Committee on Homosexual Offences and Prostitution* (London: Her Majesty's Stationery Office, 1957), Cmnd.247.

23. Ibid., para.61.

24. Sexual Offences Act 1967 (c.60), s.1(1).

25. For example, Canada decriminalised homosexuality in 1969 by virtue of s.7 of the Criminal Law Amendment Act 1968–69, Statutes of Canada 1968–69, c.38. The then Prime Minister Pierre Trudeau was quoted in John Yogis, Randall Duplak and J. Royden Trainor, *Sexual Orientation and Canadian Law: An Assessment of the Law Affecting Lesbian and Gay Persons* (Toronto: Emond Montgomery Publications, 1996), p.2, as declaring that 'the criminal law has no place in the bedrooms of the nation'.

26. As maintained by Carole J. Petersen in 'Hong Kong and the Unprecedented Transfer of Sovereignty: Values in Transition: The Development of the Gay and Lesbian Rights Movement in Hong Kong', *Loyola of Los Angeles International and Comparative Law Review*, Vol.19 (1997), p.337 at p.340, the absence in Hong Kong of legal reform on homosexuality, even after the decriminalisation of the same subject in England had taken place, was attributable to the conservative attitudes in Hong Kong and the attendant lack of public discussion and consultation on the matter.

27. *R. v. Hornby and Peaple* [1946] 2 All ER 487, per Justice Lynskey, p.488.

28. For a complete account of the MacLennan Affairs, see Sir T.L. Yang, *Report of the Commission of Inquiry into Inspector MacLennan's Case* (Hong Kong: Government Printer, 1981).

29. Law Reform Commission of Hong Kong, *Report on Laws Governing Homosexual Conduct (Topic 2)* (Hong Kong: Author, 1983).

30. Ibid., para.12.11.

31. Petersen (note 26) p.344; see also Hong Kong: *Official Report of the Proceedings of the Legislative Council (Hansard)*, (1991/ 10 July 1991), P.3, per Legislative Councillor Selina Chow Liang Shuk-Yee, p.2739.

32. See, e.g., Michael S. Duke, *The Iron House: A Memoir of the Chinese Democracy Movement and the Tiananmen Massacre* (Laton, Utah: Peregrine Smith Books, 1990); Chu-Yuan Cheng, *Behind the Tiananmen Massacre: Social, Political, and Economic Ferment in China* (Boulder, Colo.: Westview Press, 1990); Peter Li, Steven Mark, and Marjorie H. Li, *Culture and Politics in China: An Anatomy of Tiananmen Square* (New Brunswick, N.J.:

Transaction, 1991); James D. Seymour, *The International Reaction to the 1989 Crackdown in China* (New York: East Asian Institute, Columbia University, 1990).

33. Norman J. Miners, *The Government and Politics of Hong Kong* (5th ed.) (Hong Kong: Oxford University Press, 1991), p.27.

34. For events surrounding the transfer of sovereignty in 1997, see, e.g., Chris Patten, *East and West: The Last Governor of Hong Kong on Power, Freedom and the Future* (London: Pan, 1999); Joel S.K. Poon (ed.), *The Making of Special Administrative Region 1982–1997* (Hong Kong: Hong Kong Economic Times, 1997).

35. It is worth noting that the ICCPR will continue to be in force in Hong Kong by virtue of Art.39 of the Basic Law of the Hong Kong Special Administrative Region even if the Government of the People's Republic of China or of Hong Kong repeals the Hong Kong Bill of Rights Ordinance (Cap.383).

36. Hong Kong Bill of Rights Ordinance, Art.14.

37. Hong Kong (*Hansard*), (1990/ 11 July 1990), P.2, p.1964.

38. Ibid., *per* Attorney General of Hong Kong Jeremy Mathews, p.1971.

39. Hong Kong (*Hansard*) (note 31), p.2738.

40. Crimes (Amendment) Ordinance 1991.

41. Crimes Ordinance (Cap.200), s.118C.

42. Ibid., s.118F; see, in particular, sub-s.(2) thereof which states that '[a]n act which would otherwise be treated for the purposes of this section as being done in private shall not be so treated if done (a) when more than 2 persons take part or are present, or (b) in a lavatory or bathhouse to which the public have or are permitted to have access, whether on payment or otherwise.'

43. For a detailed discussion of the various inequities in the criminal law of Hong Kong with respect to sexual minorities, see Phil C. W. Chan, 'The Gay Age of Consent in Hong Kong', in *Criminal Law Forum*, Vol.15:3 (2004), forthcoming.

294. The Hong Kong Government in the *Consultative Paper* relied on certain local and overseas studies which suggested that the ratio of sexual minorities in the community was between 6 and 10 per cent of the total population which would amount to between 420,000 and 700,000 individuals in Hong Kong; see *Consultative Paper* (note 83) para.12.

295. See *Apple Daily* (note 14).

296. Wintemute (note 104) p.624.

297. Subcommittee (note 16) para.3.

298. (1986) 26 DLR (4th) 200

299. Ibid., *per* Chief Justice Dickson, p.225.

300. Carole J. Petersen, 'Implementing Equality: An Analysis of Two Recent Decisions under Hong Kong's Anti-Discrimination Laws', *Hong Kong Law Journal*, Vol.29 (1999), p.178 at p.180.

301. Art.1 of the UDHR provides that '[a]ll human beings are born free and equal in dignity and rights. They are endowed with reason and conscience and should act towards one another in a spirit of brotherhood.'

302. Kevin Reuther, 'Queer Rights Are Human Rights: Thoughts from the Back of a Cab', *Harvard Human Rights Journal*, Vol.8 (1995), p.265 at p.268.

Botswana and Swaziland's Discrimination Against Women Continues to Contribute to the HIV/AIDS Epidemic

Physicians for Human Rights

Physicians for Human Rights (PHR) is a nonprofit organization based in Cambridge, Massachusetts, composed of health professional seeking to promote the rights of all people across the globe. In the following viewpoint, PHR argues that gender inequalities are responsible for the continued prevalence of HIV/AIDS in Africa's Botswana and Swaziland. As the two countries with the highest rates of the epidemic in the world, it is imperative that the governments in these nations and international organizations do more to increase women's rights, including economic opportunities and access to medical care.

As you read, consider the following questions:

1. What percentage of HIV-positive 15–25-year-olds in sub-Saharan Africa are female?

2. What are some of the international human rights documents that have been signed or agreed to by Botswana and Swaziland?

3. What are some of the steps that Botswana and Swaziland have taken to address the HIV/AIDS epidemic?

Physicians for Human Rights, "Epidemic of Inequality: Women's Rights and HIV/AIDS in Botswana and Swaziland," physiciansforhumanrights.org, 2007, pp. 1, 13–15. Reprinted by permission.

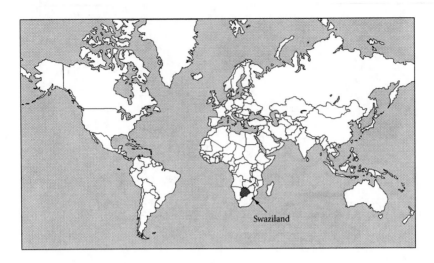

Deeply entrenched gender inequities perpetuate the HIV/
AIDS pandemic in Botswana and Swaziland, the two
countries with the highest HIV prevalence in the world. The
legal systems in both countries grant women lesser status than
men, restricting property, inheritance and other rights. Social,
economic and cultural practices create, enforce and perpetuate
legalized gender inequalities and discrimination in all aspects
of women's lives. Neither country has met its obligations under international human rights law. As a result, women continue to be disproportionately vulnerable to HIV/AIDS. This
is most starkly demonstrated by the association of gender discriminatory beliefs and sexual risk taking documented in this
report. In Botswana, participants who held three or more gender discriminatory beliefs had 2.7 times the odds of having
unprotected sex in the past year with a non-primary partner
as those who held fewer beliefs. In Swaziland, those surveyed
who held 6 or more discriminatory attitudes had twice the
odds of having multiple sexual partners than those who held
less than 6.

Despite their distinct demographic and policy profiles, the
epidemic in each country exemplifies many of the key dimen-
sions of the pandemic that is ravaging the southern African

region: an infection primarily transmitted through sexual practices rooted in women's disempowerment and lack of human rights and facilitated by poverty and food insufficiency. Young women are disproportionately affected: 75 percent of HIV-positive 15–25-year-olds in sub-Saharan Africa are female.

Conducting a population-based study in each country, Physicians for Human Rights [PHR] found four key factors contributing to women's vulnerability to HIV: 1) women's lack of control over sexual decision making, including the decision of whether to use condoms; 2) persistent HIV-related stigma and discrimination, hindering testing and engendering individuals' fears of learning their HIV status; 3) gender-discriminatory beliefs held by the majority of those surveyed—reflecting and accepting women's inferior legal, cultural and socioeconomic status—that are predictive of sexual risk taking; and 4) the failure of leadership to demonstrate the will and allocate the resources to prioritize and implement actions to promote the equality, autonomy and economic independence of women and people living with HIV/AIDS [PLWA].

In both Botswana and Swaziland, a substantial percentage of PHR community survey participants who had been tested for HIV reported that they could not refuse the test. The continuing extraordinary prevalence of HIV in Botswana, particularly among women, demonstrates that campaigns, scaled-up HIV testing, including routine testing, and antiretroviral [ARV] treatment are not enough. Women must be empowered with legal rights, sufficient food and economic opportunities to gain agency of their own lives. Men must be educated and supported to acknowledge women's equal status and throw off the yoke of socially and culturally sanctioned discriminatory beliefs and risky sexual behavior.

HIV/AIDS interventions focused solely on individual behavior will not address the factors creating vulnerability to HIV for women and men in Botswana and Swaziland, nor protect the rights and assure the well-being of those living with HIV/AIDS. National leaders, with the assistance of foreign donors and others, are obligated under international law to take immediate steps to change the unequal social, legal and economic conditions of women's lives which facilitate HIV transmission and impede testing, care and treatment. Without these immediate and comprehensive reforms, they cannot hope to halt the deadly toll of HIV/AIDS on their populations. . . .

Women must be empowered with legal rights, sufficient food and economic opportunities to gain agency of their own lives.

Human Rights Obligations

Botswana and Swaziland have acceded to, signed or ratified international human rights instruments that prohibit the disparities and abuses documented in this report and safeguard human rights essential to the prevention, care and treatment of HIV/AIDS. These include the International Covenant on Civil and Political Rights (ICCPR), the International Covenant on Economic, Social and Cultural Rights (ICESCR), the Convention on the Elimination of [All Forms of] Discrimination Against Women (Women's Convention), the Convention on the Rights of the Child, the African "Banjul" Charter on Human and Peoples' Rights and the African Charter on the Rights and Welfare of the Child.

Women's Inequality and Discrimination Against Women. International law requires the promotion of gender equality in every aspect of life. Legal equality and legal capacity "identical to that of men and the same opportunities to exercise that capacity" are explicitly required, and the rights to contract, administer property and have equal access to the justice system are singled out for special notice. The Women's Convention also directs states to eliminate discrimination against women. It obligates party states to modify their legal and cultural systems to comport with the principle of gender equality. CEDAW [Committee on the Elimination of Discrimination Against Women], the monitoring body for the Women's Convention, has issued a general recommendation that specifically speaks to the elimination of gender discrimination in the context of national AIDS policy, suggesting that countries "intensify efforts in disseminating information to increase public awareness" of HIV/AIDS in women; incorporate women's needs and rights into program planning and "give special, attention ... to the factors relating to the reproductive role of women and their subordinate position in some societies. ...."

International law requires the promotion of gender equality in every aspect of life.

This report documents numerous instances of gender inequality and discrimination. The legal systems in Botswana and Swaziland grant women lesser legal status than men, and restrict their capacity to contract and own property, among other rights. Social, economic and cultural practices create, enforce and perpetuate legalized gender inequalities and support and allow discrimination in all aspects of women's lives. The demographic profile of survey participants illustrates the various impacts of the inequitable situation of women, who are poorer and more food insufficient than men in both countries. The findings present strong evidence of how many women lack control over matters of sexuality and reproduction, including the decision whether to have sex or use condoms. This represents a failure to secure reproductive rights for women. The starkest evidence of persistent gender discrimination is the prevalence of gender discriminatory beliefs among participants in the community surveys. Furthermore, the predictive association of these beliefs with sexual risk bol-

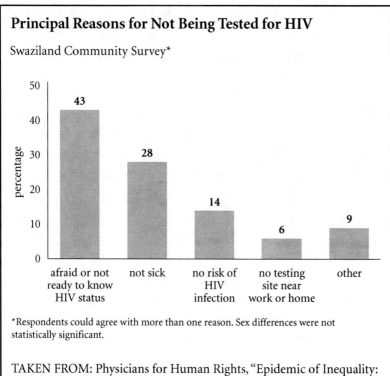

Principal Reasons for Not Being Tested for HIV

Swaziland Community Survey*

*Respondents could agree with more than one reason. Sex differences were not statistically significant.

TAKEN FROM: Physicians for Human Rights, "Epidemic of Inequality: Women's Rights and HIV/AIDS in Botswana and Swaziland," 2007. http://physiciansforhumanrights.org.

sters the conclusion that the failure to promote rights for women corresponds to a failure of these governments to comply with the obligation to protect women, and men, from potential HIV infection, among other harms.

Discrimination Against PLWA. Discrimination based on any ground is prohibited under human rights law, including "race, color, sex, language, religion, political or other opinion, natural or social origin, property, birth or other status." The UN [United Nations] Commission on Human Rights has explicitly confirmed that health status, including HIV/AIDS, is a prohibited basis for discrimination. The study findings demonstrate that discrimination on the basis of HIV status occurs in

Botswana and Swaziland. The absence of legislation specifically protecting the rights of those living with HIV/AIDS, in addition to educational or other measures, speaks to the governments' failure to protect the rights of PLWA. As the study findings show, the perceived need for secrecy and projected fears of being stigmatized and experiencing bad treatment should an individual test positive for HIV have clear implications for whether individuals will take preventive measures and seek testing or care. As with gender discriminatory beliefs, affirmatively addressing these fears is the responsibility of states charged with ensuring equality for those within its borders.

Failure to Progressively Realize the Right to Health. In conferring the obligation to ensure the right to health, the ICESCR states that "[t]he States Parties to the present Covenant recognize the right of everyone to the enjoyment of the highest attainable standard of physical and mental health." Among other obligations, states must take steps to realize "[t]he prevention, treatment and control of epidemic, endemic . . . and other diseases" and "[t]he creation of conditions which would assure to all medical service and medical attention in the event of sickness."

In General Comment 14 to the ICESCR, the UN Committee on Economic, Social and Cultural Rights (ESC Rights Committee) explained that the right to health "is closely related to and dependent on the realization of other human rights . . ." set forth in the Universal Declaration of Human Rights and the two covenants. It "embraces a wide range of socioeconomic factors that promote conditions in which people can lead a healthy life, and extends to the underlying determinants of health," such as access to food and water, sanitation, housing, and health-promoting labor and environmental conditions. Popular participation in all levels of decision making regarding health is an aspect of the right, which encompasses availability, accessibility, acceptability and quality.

In many respects, for example the persistent food insufficiency, economic deprivation and gender inequality described previously, Swaziland is not meeting its right to health obligations. The survey and the interviews describe a situation where a significant proportion of participants, in particular women and PLWA, lack access to sufficient food, safe living conditions and a secure work situation, which translate into an elevated risk of becoming infected with HIV or being less able to cope with positive status. Swaziland community survey participants fault leadership across the board for failing to support people infected or affected with HIV/AIDS with subsistence levels of food, water, shelter and land and to spend sufficient resources on HIV prevention. Swaziland's obligations under the ICESCR require that the government take such steps to implement its national HIV/AIDS policy, and in particular, adopt a gender perspective in terms of both strategy and implementation.

Denial of the Right to Life. The ICCPR states: "[e]very human being has the inherent right to life. This right shall be protected by law. No one shall be arbitrarily deprived of his life." In General Comment 6, the Human Rights Committee, monitor of the ICCPR, stated that positive measures to protect the right to life include interventions to reduce infant mortality and increase life expectancy and "especially . . . to eliminate malnutrition and epidemics."

It should be evident that the drivers and impacts of the HIV/AIDS epidemic detailed in this report fall squarely within the mandate of the protection of the right to life. In order to meet their obligations under the ICCPR, affirmative measures must be taken by Botswana and Swaziland to correct food insufficiency; lack of correct information about HIV prevention and transmission; lack of access and literacy concerning lifesaving ARV treatment; and the persistence of gender and HIV-related discrimination that increase vulnerability to HIV/AIDS. While both countries, and in particular Botswana, have taken steps to address the epidemic, for example by establishing testing and treatment programs, the study findings identified persistent gaps in these programs, as evidenced by the proportions of community respondents who had not tested for HIV. Moreover, survey participants in both countries identified their leaders' failure to take positive measures, as required by the ICCPR, to address the pandemic.

Remedial actions are urgent and essential if women in Botswana and Swaziland are to gain control over their lives.

Donor States' and International Organizations' Obligations. Human rights obligations are not only borne by states to their own citizens. Under the human rights framework, third parties, including foreign donors, corporations, and international and intergovernmental organizations, also have obligations not to violate rights nor impede their realization, and to structure their aid policies and programs consonant with the protection of rights. The ESC Rights Committee has noted that this obligation rests with all States under international law, and is particularly the responsibility of more developed countries.

The US, through PEPFAR [President's Emergency Plan for AIDS Relief] and other aid programs, and the UN agencies, among other donors to Botswana and Swaziland, are obliged under international human rights law to assist Botswana and Swaziland to address the failures discussed here. In particular, it is incumbent on these third parties to encourage immediate measures to reform discriminatory laws and enact protections for women and PLWA; to provide funds and technical assistance for legal aid, sustainable food programs and the scaling-up of HIV testing and treatment; and to facilitate capacity building and cooperation between the governments and civil society in each country and in the region. Without such efforts, fragmented and uncoordinated aid and policies may create obstacles to remedial interventions by the countries to address the human rights abuses that perpetuate the HIV/ AIDS pandemic.

In the struggle to prevent HIV and alleviate the suffering caused by the AIDS pandemic, realization of human rights is imperative and essential, particularly for women who bear the brunt of the epidemic. Botswana and Swaziland, though different in many respects, are accountable for failing to meet many of the same human rights obligations. The study findings describe the deleterious impacts of gender inequality and discrimination, discrimination on the basis of HIV-positive status, failure to provide essential information and access to HIV testing and treatment, and the life-threatening consequences of the lack of adequate food to meet basic needs, particularly for women. Implementation of the recommendations outlined in this report will be challenging, requiring prioritization, resources and political will, but remedial actions are urgent and essential if women in Botswana and Swaziland are to gain control over their lives and freedom from the threat of HIV/AIDS.

In Thailand, Transsexuals Are Discriminated Against

Jason Armbrecht

Jason Armbrecht is a coauthor of Frommer's Southeast Asia, *a guide to the region. In the following viewpoint, he argues that transsexuals are discriminated against in Thailand. Despite the prevalence of transsexuals in the country, they are given little protection under the law, he says. They cannot legally change their gender on official identity cards, nor can they marry a member of the same sex. Armbrecht asserts that Buddhist beliefs may play a role in how transsexuals are received and urges a change in cultural views about this ever-growing population.*

As you read, consider the following questions:

1. When was the first transsexual surgery performed in Thailand?
2. What percentage of Thailand is Buddhist?
3. What happens to the assets of the deceased when a transsexual's partner dies?

Walk down almost any busy street in Thailand, especially in a tourist hot spot such as Bangkok, Pattaya or Phuket, and chances are good that you will see at least one Thai transsexual. Thailand's first sex change surgery was performed in 1972 and the country now hosts more of these pro-

Jason Armbrecht, "Transsexuals in Thai Law," *Thai Law Forum*, April 11, 2008. http://www.thailawforum.com/. Reprinted by permission.

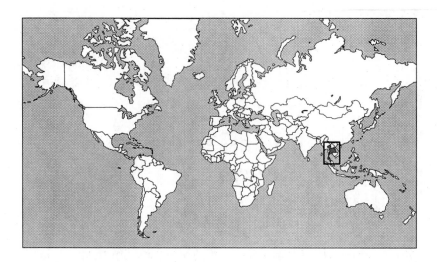

cedures per year than any other country in the world. Estimates on the current number of Thai transsexuals range from 10,000 to 100,000, including a number of pop singers and television and movie stars. A transsexual beauty pageant, the Miss Tiffany's Universe, is televised nationally each year. On the surface, Thailand appears to live up to its worldwide reputation as a place where transsexuals can experience greater freedom and acceptance than other nations. It would seem curious then that Thai laws are in actuality quite conservative regarding transsexuals and their rights. A closer look at Thai society and culture, however, reveals a society with a decidedly mixed view of transsexuals—a view reflected in a legal system that does not afford transsexuals many of the rights and protections enjoyed by the rest of the population.

Thailand is roughly 95% Buddhist and as such, the issue of transsexuals in Thai society may be examined through this lens. Unlike Christians, Buddhists cannot point to specific religious laws or teachings forbidding homosexuality, transsexuals or gay marriage. One of the fundamental teachings of Buddhism is tolerance of those who act differently or hold different views. At first blush, this tolerance (if not acceptance) would seem to extend to transsexuals in Thailand. Transsexuals are integrated into everyday life and physical or verbal assault on transsexuals in public is extremely rare.

This patina of tolerance is also borne out in a survey of male to female transsexuals conducted by Dr. Sam Winter, associate professor, Division of Learning, Development and Diversity, Faculty of Education at the University of Hong Kong. According to his findings, the transsexuals polled indicated that 40% of their fathers and 66% of their mothers either accepted or were encouraging when told of their decision to change genders, numbers he believes would be impossible to duplicate in the West.

Unfortunately for transsexuals, this familial tolerance does not mirror the opinion of certain sections of Thai society in relation to what legal protections should be afforded transsexuals. Nearly 70% of respondents in a Ramkhamhaeng University public opinion center poll disapproved of legalizing gay marriage or allowing transsexuals to legally adopt their new gender on ID cards and passports.

Recent history demonstrates how quickly this type of prejudice can lead to institutional discrimination.

The obvious question arises: If transsexuals are such a visible part of everyday Thai life, and are clearly tolerated by society, then why do some polls indicate that a majority of Thais oppose granting transsexuals the broad spectrum of legal protection that other nations (the Netherlands and Belgium for example) have afforded transsexuals? These rights include legally changing their gender on public identity cards, the right to civil unions and employment protection rights. Again, Buddhism may play a role. While the Buddhist focus on tolerance does in part shape Thai society's tolerant view of transsexuals, the Buddhist principle of karma may provide an alternative explanation. Karmicly speaking, we are all paying off debts accrued through actions in past lives. Many Thais view transsexuals' lives as generally unhappy and unfulfilling. Some also deem that this unhappiness is the result of a karmic punishment forced on them by sexual misdeeds in past lives. The standard karmic tale is that transsexuals were formerly 'playboys' in their former lives and, as a result of breaking so many lovelorn hearts of women, were imposed the ultimate punishment: making them a woman trapped in a man's body, forever doomed to unrequited love. Therefore, they are a group to be pitied, not protected.

A fundamental misunderstanding of the nature of transsexuality might also contribute. There is a dearth of Thai language materials focused on educating the public about transsexuality. According to a 2003 study by Dr. Winter, 51% of university students agreed with the statement '(transsexuals) are men with something wrong with their mind.' Considering these are ostensibly well-educated and open-minded young people, one can only imagine what the percentage would be if the rest of Thai society was polled.

Recent history demonstrates how quickly this type of prejudice can lead to institutional discrimination. In December 1996, a transsexual student enrolled in the education program at a public university murdered a female friend. In response, another well-known higher education institution in charge of Thailand's teaching universities banned transgender and homosexual students from attending their teacher training facilities. Transsexuals were variously referred to as 'sexually deviant' and 'sick . . . mentally' by members of the institute, and considered a bad influence on children. This argument was simply keeping in line with the Department of Mental Health, which at the time considered homosexuality a mental disorder. Subsequent pressure from both Thai and Western gay rights groups soon forced a repeal of the ban.

As far as the Thai government is concerned, male to female transsexuals are legally men. Transsexuals cannot legally change their gender on their ID cards, leading to problems with potential employers. Many employers do not want possible complications involved with hiring a transsexual if an equally qualified 'normal' person can be hired. Because of this, the vast majority are relegated to occupations traditionally held by women, i.e., waitresses, hairdressers, makeup artists, and vendors, even if they are university graduates. Transsexuals' birth gender must remain the same on their passports as well, a fact which can lead to confusion and unwanted scrutiny at border crossings and immigration checkpoints. Thailand also prohibits same-sex marriage, meaning that when the partner of a transsexual dies, the deceased's family receives any and all assets.

There have been some positive developments, however, as the past six years have seen important legal gains for transsexuals and the gay community in general. In 2002, the Department of Mental Health, under intense pressure from the gay community, removed homosexuality from its list of mental disorders. This decision helped pave the way for the Thai military to announce in 2005 that it would discontinue its practice of dismissing transsexual and gay recruits for having 'a severe mental disorder,' and the subsequent announcement in March 2008 that the military would be adding a 'third category' for transsexuals. This third category would allow transsexuals to be dismissed from service due to 'an illness that cannot be cured in thirty days,' thereby removing the scarlet letter of 'mental disorder' from their service records—records that must be provided at each job interview and with each loan application. 2007 saw the legislature expand the legal definition of rape from a man who forcibly has sex with someone to whom he is not legally married, to include forcible sex perpetrated by either sex against either sex. Before this change, a man who raped a transsexual could only be charged (if he was indeed even charged) with sexual molestation, a crime resulting in a fine. Offenders under the new law face the prospect of four to twenty years in jail.

Detailed Map of Thailand

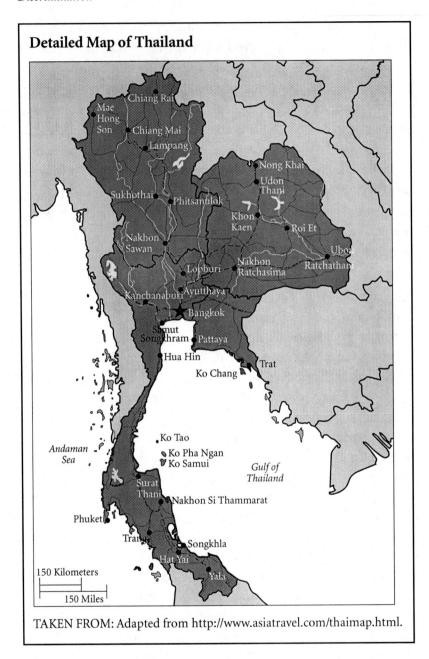

TAKEN FROM: Adapted from http://www.asiatravel.com/thaimap.html.

With the September 2006 coup, the Thai military, perhaps counterintuitively, provided the transsexual and gay communities their best chance to date of gaining constitutional protections. After the Council for National Security suspended the constitution, gay and lesbian rights groups such as the Anjaree Foundation, the first effective lesbian rights organization in Thailand, and the Gay Political Group of Thailand began lobbying the Constitutional Drafting Committee and the Constitutional Drafting Assembly to add language assuring protections for transgender, gay and lesbian citizens. A proposal to add the term 'sexual diversities' to the list of groups covered under the equality clause (Section 30) of the draft constitution was debated, but ultimately voted down by a 54 to 23 margin. A well-known transsexual advocate believes that semantics played a role in the defeat of the proposal. Speaking to the International Gay and Lesbian Human Rights Commission, she noted, 'The fact that we do not have neutral words in the official Thai language was used by some Assembly members to sideline the importance of extending the equality and protection against discrimination for LGBT (lesbian, gay, bisexual and transsexual) people.' The LGBT community and academics have been trying to develop new terms regarding sexual orientation and the Thai word meaning 'sexual diversities' may have been confusing to some Assembly members, she said.

Their social and legal status in Thailand, even when compared to the rest of the LGBT community, is unique.

The 2007 constitution, as currently written, states that 'The Thai people, irrespective of their origins, sexes or religions, shall enjoy equal protection under this Constitution' (Section 5) and 'Unjust discrimination against a person on the grounds of the difference in origin, race, language, sex, age, disability, physical or health condition, personal status, economic or social standing, religious belief, education or constitutionally political view, shall not be permitted' (Section 30). Although transsexuals and homosexuals are not explicitly mentioned, there are signs that transsexuals and homosexuals will be actively using the new constitution as a basis for defending themselves against discrimination. Late last year, a leading proponent of the Gay Political Group of Thailand claimed that he was refused a life insurance policy by an insurance company due to his homosexuality. After meeting with the Constitution Drafting Council, who agreed that the company was violating his constitutional rights, he threatened legal action and petitioned the Commerce Ministry and the Office of the Insurance Commission (OIC), resulting in a certification from the OIC and the insurance company that homosexuals are guaranteed the right to purchase insurance policies.

While this case shows that the new constitution can and will be used by the gay and transsexual community to assert their rights, it is interesting to note that the concessions granted by the OIC and the insurance company do not cover transsexuals. This fact illuminates a problem facing transsexuals—while their plight may be more misunderstood by the general public and their path towards true equality more complex than the homosexual community's, they have not yet formed an advocacy group focused solely on furthering their agenda. This might be due in part to Thai society's traditional insistence on harmony and avoiding public confrontations. Advocacy and protests by gay and lesbian groups such as Anjaree and the Gay Political Group of Thailand have resulted in transsexuals' recent legal gains. Their social and legal status in Thailand, even when compared to the rest of the LGBT community, is unique. As such, further gains may require forceful advocacy by transsexual groups. As the advocate for a gay advocacy group in Thailand observes, 'The situation is very bad for gays but for transgenders, it's even worse.'

Saudi Arabian Women Are Not Equally Represented in the Workforce

Ed Attwood

Ed Attwood is the deputy editor of Arabian Business, *a comprehensive guide to Middle East business and Persian Gulf industry news. In the following viewpoint, Attwood highlights the findings of a study by a female senior adviser of a local think tank. The study finds that only 15 percent of the Saudi workforce is made up of women. As a result, the author of the study calls for the Saudi government to institute legislation to create employment opportunities for women and to promote equal participation by women in the labor market. Illiteracy in rural areas contributes to the underemployment of women. Most women who are employed have jobs in the public, rather than the private, sector.*

As you read, consider the following questions:

1. To what does the author of the study attribute skepticism toward the idea of women in the workforce?
2. How has the participation of women in the Saudi workforce changed since 1992?
3. What percentage of the public sector employment is made up of women? Of the private sector?

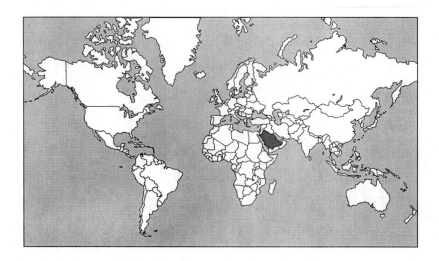

Saudi Arabia is being held back by its failure to tap the female labour force, a recent study has warned.

The research—called 'Women's Employment in Saudi Arabia: A Major Challenge'—reveals that only fifteen percent of
the Saudi workforce is made up of women.

"Since women's role within Saudi society has traditionally
been that of wife and mother, the move toward greater female
participation in the labor force has been met with skepticism,
debate and even hostility," said author Mona Al-Munajjed, a
senior adviser with a local Booz & Company think tank, the
Ideation Center.

"To this end, the Saudi government needs to ratify, enforce
and implement legislation that promotes equal participation
in the labour market, implement policies that create employment opportunities for women, and establish institutional
mechanisms that promote women's well-being and success in
the workforce."

The report added that major reforms were needed—not
only in Saudi Arabia but across the Arab world—if countries
were to develop into full market economies.

Since 1992, the percentage of women participating in the
Saudi workforce has nearly tripled from 5.4 percent to 14.4

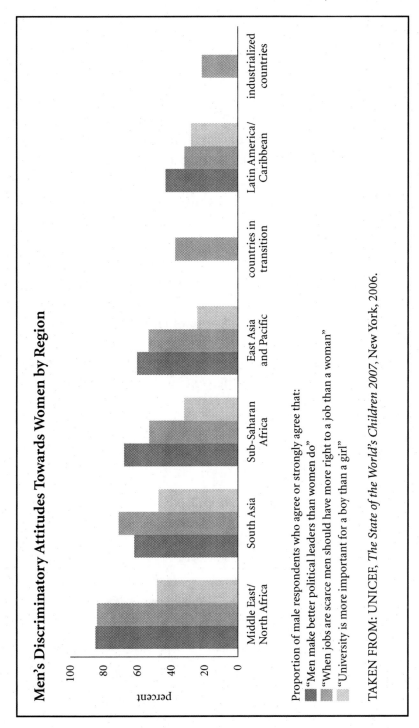

Men's Discriminatory Attitudes Towards Women by Region

Proportion of male respondents who agree or strongly agree that:

"Men make better political leaders than women do"

"When jobs are scarce men should have more right to a job than a woman"

"University is more important for a boy than a girl"

TAKEN FROM: UNICEF, *The State of the World's Children 2007*, New York, 2006.

percent, although this still compares dismally with the UAE [United Arab Emirates] rate of 59 percent.

Illiteracy is also a major barrier in rural communities, the research also indicated. According to UNESCO [United Nations Educational, Scientific and Cultural Organization], in 2007, 20.6 percent of Saudi women over the age of 15 were illiterate, leaving a total of one million women completely unable to enter the labour market due to a lack of skills.

20.6 percent of Saudi women over the age of 15 were illiterate, leaving a total of one million women completely unable to enter the labour market due to a lack of skills.

The public sector is by far the largest employer of Saudi women, who make up 30 percent of the workforce. Only five percent of Saudi working women are employed in the private sector, the report stated.

From a management perspective, the research note also claimed that less than one percent of decision-making posts are held by women.

New Zealand's Male Nurses Are Often Discriminated Against Because They Are Perceived to Be Gay

Thomas Harding

In the following viewpoint excerpt Thomas Harding, a professor of health at Høgskolen i Buskerud in Drammen, Norway, argues that male nurses in New Zealand are unfairly stereotyped as gay. Unfortunately, this stereotyping leads to discrimination at multiple levels, including in the hiring and promotional processes. In addition, male nurses are often shunned by female nurses and patients, who erroneously believe that gay men are sexual predators. Harding urges the nursing community to break this stereotype in order to encourage more men, gay and straight, to become caretakers.

As you read, consider the following questions:

1. According to Harding, what are two popular beliefs about men in nursing, especially gay male nurses?
2. What is internalized homophobia, as described by Harding?
3. Which group of male nurses was more likely to experience difficultly with accepting homosexuality?

Thomas Harding, "The Construction of Men Who Are Nurses as Gay," *Journal of Advanced Nursing*, vol. 60, no. 6, 2007, pp. 636–637, 639–641, 642–643, notes 643–644. Reproduced by permission.

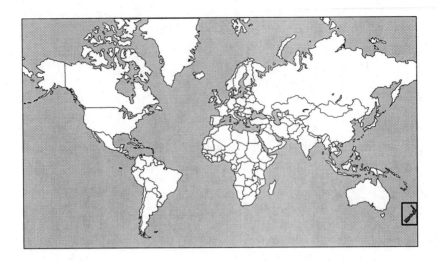

Numerous authors have described the construction of nursing as women's work (for example, Armstrong 2002, Evans 2004, Evertsson & Lindqvist 2005, Holroyd *et al* 2002, Miers 2000, Okrainec 1994, Porter-O'Grady 2001, Romen & Anson 2005). The geographical diversity reflected in these studies ranging across the United States of America (USA), Europe, the Middle East, Asia and Oceania reveals this as a global discourse.

An accompanying discourse stereotyping male nurses as gay is also described by many authors in a variety of specific cultural contexts (for example, Bohan 1997, Isaacs & Poole 1996, Meadus 2000, Williams 1995). According to Salvage (1985, p. 24), 'there does appear to be a higher proportion of gay men in nursing than in the male population at large, although of course there are no figures to prove it'.

Nursing is part of a larger culture; therefore, it is to be expected that it will reflect societal values. A predominant value is heterosexism, i.e., the belief that 'the only right, natural, normal, god-given, and therefore privileged way of relating to each other is heterosexually' (Gray *et al.* 1996, p. 205). Heterosexism underpins the homophobia which has been found to be widespread in nursing (Richmond & McKenna 1998). . . .

Persistence of the Stereotype of the Gay Male Nurse

All participants stated that in their experience the majority of men in nursing are heterosexual. According to Allan, 'it has definitely been my experience that most male nurses are not gay, but I think public perception is still that most male nurses are gay'. This was confirmed by all the others. For example, Bruce recalled the comment: 'you'd better watch out for them, you know what they're like!' He described the context:

> A guy who had broken one of his legs needed a urinal and he rang the bell . . . and I remember a visitor, a guy, walked past and said to him, when he saw me with the bottle as I started to pull the curtains, 'you'd better watch out for them, you know what they're like'.

I think the public perception is still that most male nurses are gay.

He believed that the comment implied that as a man and a nurse he was gay. In fact, the comment illustrates two popular beliefs. First, men in nursing are gay; Martin described the prevailing stereotype when he entered nursing in 1969, 'you were queer, I think the word is, alcoholic or religious'. This stereotype persists, as evidenced by Phillip, a student nurse at the time of the interviews, who had 'heard the stereotypical comments that, "yeah, you must be gay if you want to be a nurse"'. Second, homosexual men are sexual predators; the implication of the comment 'you know what they're like' is that homosexual men are intent on either seducing or sexually assaulting young men. It was the second of these two implications that disturbed him most:

> I just found it abhorrent that he actually thought someone, irrespective of sexuality really, would use a situation involving the client in such a perverse way. I find that appalling.

Grant described it as 'interesting' that such beliefs exist and are commented on, as when he announced his decision to become a nurse:

Lots of people still had this image of male nurses being homosexuals. My doctor actually passed a comment when I told him. He was quite excited about it: 'it'll be nice to have some heterosexual males in the workforce'.

Allan hid his homosexuality. The association of men, nursing and homosexuality was too strong for him to tell his parents that he had applied for nursing school: 'my being a nurse was not about my sexuality, but I thought that people would think that it was; that I would be identified as gay'.

One of the interesting features of this construction is that it applies only to men who are general nurses. Both Luke and Bart, who were psychiatric nurses, noted this paradox. Luke commented: 'one of my perceptions was that most men who went into the general system were gay. That was fairly accepted'.

Meeting Homophobia

Both Robert and Charles, who are gay, have been told 'you're a waste' by female colleagues. Rather than directly challenging the inherent heterosexism, they both made light of such remarks. Charles responded 'it's not wasted', while Robert ignored them: 'it doesn't bother me. That sort of stuff makes me aware of their lack of understanding and insight into how they treat other people'. Usually such remarks were not consciously ill intentioned; however, Andrew had cause to file a complaint against a female staff member for sexual harassment after she commented to colleagues, 'we don't want more of that sort here' with respect to his homosexuality.

Two participants identified that internalized homophobia, the internalized negative attitudes that some homosexuals experience, had been problematic for them. Warren described the personal impact:

There I was hiding my sexuality and in hiding my sexuality I picked up ideas of not being as good as anybody else and other people are much better than me and all this kind of stuff, and not being proud of who I was because underneath it all I had these ideas I was squashing. . . . I was hiding my sexuality. Where do you pin it all? Being gay must be evil and bad and all the rest of it and 'oh, my God, I think I'm gay!' So I focused my energy on being straight, but underneath it all I know I'm bad and evil and all the rest of it.

In the quote above, his choice of the present tense, 'I know' rather than the past tense form 'knew' could indicate that internalized homophobia continued to influence his feelings of self-worth. He raised issues of moral judgment; in line 6 equating being gay with 'evil' and 'bad' and reiterated this in line 8. The use of the word 'evil' can also have religious connotations and Mark recalled a classmate, saying, 'you're a sinner, you know'. Warren and Mark were caught in the complex node where homophobia, religious beliefs and moral values intersect.

Both Robert and Charles, who are gay, have been told 'you're a waste' by female colleagues.

Warren talked about 'hiding' his sexuality (line 5) in the above quote. This was explored further in the interview; he expressed 'the fear of being outed', or having his sexuality known by the patients:

I always felt awkward around younger men, like in orthopaedics. But I wonder if the phobia, almost, of working with young men is that they might call me gay and that would be too confronting.

Warren's 'awkwardness' resulted from feeling 'other' and the concomitant feelings of shame, or as he said from 'not being proud of who I was'. He hid his sexuality, but the fear of being identified as gay created considerable tension for him.

The reaction of patients to his sexuality created tension for Andrew when he was a young nurse: 'a seven-bedded room with young male footballers all in traction was my worst nightmare . . . because I just felt vulnerable that I stood out'.

The hegemonic discourse of heterosexual masculinity can create a fear that homosexuality is a barrier to career progression. After he had 'come out' Allan was advised, by a lesbian colleague in a more senior position, that openness about his sexuality would hinder his career progression:

> I was interested in a charge nurse position and I sought advice from another senior colleague in the hospital who had abilities in coaching and practice at interviewing. She believed the fact people were aware that I was gay was going to be something that went against me.

Allan was not appointed; however, on reflection he thought the decision was not owing to his sexuality, but that the better candidate was appointed.

The hegemonic discourse of heterosexual masculinity can create a fear that homosexuality is a barrier to career progression.

Ian, however, gave an example in which homophobia did have an impact on a career in nursing:

> There may be one or two [gay men] who were quite flamboyant in their behaviour, but some of my colleagues were quite critical, the more assertive ones, the more masculine ones maybe, they were very critical of these people . . . they never really completed their training.
>
> *Interviewer*: So the other men were quite critical.
>
> *Ian*: Yes, if they were seen to be that way inclined. I mean, I know for a fact, in recent years some of those who may have been critical were probably gay themselves.

Strategies to Protect One's Heterosexuality

Several of the heterosexual respondents reported their comfort about working alongside gay men and about being presumed gay. For example, Paul in response to the question, 'did it bother you, the fact that people might have questioned your sexuality?' replied, 'no, it didn't bother me at all . . . I've got nothing against gays, so I don't perceive it as being a value judgment on me whether people think I'm gay or not'. Ian, however, avoided contact with known gay colleagues: 'I personally didn't see it as a problem; if they kept themselves to themselves that's fine, and [if] there was nothing flamboyant on duty'.

Edward and Bruce emphasized their heterosexuality to avoid the assumption of homosexuality:

> In my early years as a nurse before I started to become relaxed with who I was, there were times when I would overtly state the more masculine things that I did. I wanted people to know *I* was a man. I used to play senior rugby, and I did mountain climbing and I was a farmer. (Edward)

For Edward, the issue was complex. He acknowledged that being a rugby player and a farmer was not a protection as 'there are gays everywhere', but he found it difficult to be thought of as homosexual because of his strong Christian beliefs:

> It is not until I have become confident about who I am that it then doesn't worry me what other people want to judge, but before that it did. . . . It's not straightforward, and to simplify it hooks back into my fundamentalist Christian [beliefs] and to unravel that stuff becomes particularly convoluted.

Edward occupied an uncomfortable and contradictory position. On one hand, he identified himself as 'tolerant' and considered society to be more so, yet also identified as having fundamentalist Christian beliefs: beliefs which are generally not compatible with acceptance, or tolerance, of homosexuality. Bruce also owned strong Christian beliefs; however, they were not part of a need to be identified as heterosexual. For him it was about the avoidance of harassment:

> I deliberately wore a wedding ring—particularly in coronary care.

> *Interviewer*: Why?

> *Bruce*: Because I got sick of all the comments from my colleagues.

> *Interviewer*: What sort of comments?

> *Bruce*: Just the comments, the looks, the snide remarks—always questioning. I had a number of people say to me, 'you're married now, that's great!' I deliberately did that because I got to the point where, 'oh, look, I don't have to put up with this!'

> *Interviewer*: What were they making these comments about?

> *Bruce*: Issues of sexuality. . . .

Homophobia and Nursing

Salvage (1985) argued that gay men might feel more comfortable being open about their sexuality within the nursing milieu:

> It might be that male nurses, having decided to enter a predominantly female occupation feel more able to be open about their sexual preferences. . . . Or perhaps they are attracted to it because it does not seem to demand the macho attributes of masculine stereotyping. (p. 24)

There is ample evidence, both in the literature and from the participants in my study, to dispute any claim that nursing offers a safe environment within which to disclose one's homosexuality. Gay male patients' experiences of meeting homophobia are well documented (for example, Hayter 1996, Holyoake 2001, Kelly *et al.* 1988, Platzer 1993, Richmond & McKenna 1998, Taylor & Robertson 1994).

My participants revealed that openly gay nurses also are subjected to homophobia. While some of the expression is overt, much is covert. None of the participants expressed overt homophobia; nonetheless, the phrases used, such as 'not seeing it as a problem if there was nothing flamboyant' or 'if they kept themselves to themselves', are salient. They reveal an expectation that gay colleagues will behave in a manner that others determine as appropriate. Gray *et al.* (1996) described this phenomenon in their discussion of heterosexism in nursing education:

> People often say to nonheterosexuals, 'why can't you just keep your sex life private?' This communicates a view that lesbian and gay existence is only about sex, that (homosexual) sex is an unacceptable topic and practice, and that if one is engaging in such practices, one should have the decency to keep it quiet. The message is clear—keep quiet and remain invisible. (p. 208)

Gray *et al.* (1996, p. 208) also found that lesbian nursing educators and graduate students were treated differently and that they were subject to 'lesbian phobia'. Therefore, the warning one of the present participants received from a lesbian colleague that his openness would be detrimental to his career prospects may be well-founded in her own and others' experiences.

An interesting feature of the interviews was that the men who described the most difficulty in accepting homosexuality were those who identified as gay. This reflects the insidious nature of homophobia and the difficulty that gay men face in overcoming the conditioning of internalized homophobia. For some, this may compel them to participate in homophobic activities to remain hidden. They spend considerable amounts of time monitoring themselves to ensure that they cannot be suspected of homosexuality (Hoffman & Bakken 2001). Ian's example, cited above, that those who may have been 'critical were probably gay themselves' are illustrative of what Buchbinder (1998, p. 126) described as a dual dynamic: *'the fascination of the possibility of same-sex attraction* and, simultaneously, *its prohibition and persecution'*. The language often used underscores the otherness of gay men: 'these people' and 'that way inclined'. Such a use of language illustrates Foucault's (1972) thesis that discourses are constructed as a means of regulation.

To be the homosexual 'other' in the heterosexual/homosexual binary positions one as a less-valued member of society and limits access to the privileges of the dominant group. Comments such as 'you're a waste', directed to gay colleagues by female nurses, are generally well-meaning, ignorant of the inherent heterosexism, but they perpetrate the discourse that non-subscription to hegemonic heterosexuality is a 'lack'. The stigma associated with the stereotype of the gay male nurse is compounded by the image of gay men as deviants and sexual predators (Levine 1992). This is a challenging position for heterosexual men, as members of the dominant gender group, to occupy and no doubt contributes to the need, described by some of the participants, to affirm their masculinity, i.e., heterosexuality. . . .

By choosing a workplace role that is considered unmanly they become associated with effeminateness and homosexuality.

Conclusion

Heterosexuality continues to govern global culture, and discrimination remains part of the everyday experience of gay and lesbian people worldwide. Such discrimination, which includes political and cultural exclusion, cultural abuse, legal violence, street violence, economic discrimination and personal boycotts, positions homosexual masculinities at the bottom of the masculine gender hierarchy.

Within this framework, men entering stereotypical female occupations, such as nursing, do not conform to the script of hegemonic masculinity and risk having their gender identity questioned. By choosing a workplace role that is considered unmanly they become associated with effeminateness and homosexuality. Within such a matrix male nurses construct both their masculine and professional identities and experience gender.

This has important implications for the profession. Nonsexual touch is fundamental to the provision of care, but discourses which stereotype male nurses as gay and conflate homosexuality and sexual predation create a potent barrier to the provision of care for other men. The continuing stigma associated with homosexuality may deter the entry of more men into nursing, and the experience of homophobia in a profession which espouses an ethic of care may be a significant issue in the retention of male practitioners. Nurses need to be challenged to address their collusion in stigmatizing discourses.

In a changing recruitment context, the profession seeks to encourage more men into the profession, including those from minority backgrounds, who are already marginalized with respect to hegemonic masculinity. Nursing education can play a pivotal role in helping men in the profession understand and resist the sociopolitical constraints that shape their experience, and perpetrate gender and sexual stereotypes which oppress and marginalize both women and men.

References

Anonymous. (2001) Where are all the male nurses? *Australian Nursing Journal* 9(3), 35.

Armstrong F. (2002) Not just women's business: men in nursing. *Australian Nursing Journal* 9(11), 24–26.

Bohan J.S. (1997) Regarding gender: essentialism, constructionism, and feminist psychology. In *Toward a New Psychology of Gender. A Reader* (Gergen M.M. & Davis S.N., eds), Routledge, New York, pp. 31–48.

Brannon R. (1976) The male sex role: our culture's blueprint of manhood and what it's done for us lately. In *The Forty-Nine Percent Majority: The Male Sex Role* (David D.S. & Brannon R., eds), Addison-Wesley, Reading, MA, pp. 1–48.

Buchbinder D. (1998) *Performance Anxieties: Reproducing Masculinity.* Allen & Unwin, St Leonards, Australia.

Burman E. (1991) What discourse is not. *Philosophical Psychology* 4(3), 325–342.

Burr V. (1995) *An Introduction to Social Construction.* Routledge, London.

Butler J. (1990) *Gender Trouble: Feminism and the Subversion of Identity.* Routledge, New York.

Connell R.W. (1995) *Masculinities.* Allen & Unwin, St Leonards, Australia.

Evans J. (2004) Men nurses: a historical and feminist perspective. *Journal of Advanced Nursing* 47(3), 321–328.

Evertsson L. & Lindqvist R. (2005) Welfare state and women's work: the professional projects of nurses and occupational therapists in Sweden. *Nursing Inquiry* 12(4), 256–268.

Foucault M. (1972) *The Archeology of Knowledge* (A. M. S. Smith, Trans.). Tavistock, London.

Gergen K.J. (1999) *An Introduction to Social Construction.* Sage, London.

Gramsci A. (1974) *Selections from the Prison Notebooks* (G. C. Spivak, Trans.). The Johns Hopkins University Press, Baltimore, MD.

Gray D.P., Kramer M., Minick P., McGehe L., Thomas D. & Greiner D. (1996) Heterosexism in nursing education. *Journal of Nursing Education* 35, 204–210.

Hayter M. (1996) Is non-judgemental care possible in the context of nurses' attitudes to patients' sexuality? *Journal of Advanced Nursing* 24, 662–666.

Hoffman A. & Bakken L. (2001) Are educational and life experiences related to homophobia? *Educational Research Quarterly* 24(4), 67–82.

Holroyd E.A., Bond M.H. & Chan H.Y. (2002) Perceptions of sex-role stereotypes, self-concept, and nursing role ideal in Chinese nursing students. *Journal of Advanced Nursing* 37(3), 294–303.

Holyoake D.-D. (2001) *The Male Nurse: Addressing the Myths of Maleness in Nursing.* APS Publishing, Salisbury, UK.

Howarth D. (2000) *Discourse.* Open University Press, Buckingham, UK.

Isaacs D. & Poole M. (1996) Being a man and becoming a nurse: three men's stories. *Journal of Gender Studies* 5(1), 39–47.

Kelly J.A., Lawrence J.S., Hood H.V., Smith S. & Cook D.J. (1988) Nurses' attitudes toward AIDS. *Journal of Continuing Education in Nursing* 19(12), 28–38.

Kimmel M.S. (1997) Masculinity as homophobia: Fear, shame and silence in the construction of gender. In *Toward a New Psychology of Gender* (Gergen M.M. & Davis S.N., eds), Routledge, New York, pp. 223–244.

King J.R. (1999) Am not! Are too! Using queer standpoint in postmodern critical ethnography. *Qualitative Studies in Education* 12(5), 473–490.

Krane V. (2001) One lesbian feminist epistemology: integrating feminist standpoint, queer theory, and feminist cultural studies. *The Sports Psychologist* 15, 401–411.

Levine M. (1992) The status of gay men in the workplace. In *Men's Lives* (Kimmel M. & Messner M., eds), 2nd edn. Maxwell Macmillan, Toronto, Canada, pp. 251–266.

Lincoln Y.S. & Guba E.G. (1985) *Naturalistic Inquiry*. Sage, Newbury Park, CA.

Marcus G.E. (1994) What comes (just) after 'post'? The case of ethnography. In *Handbook of Qualitative Research* (Denzin N.K. & Lincoln Y.S., eds), Sage, Thousand Oaks, CA, pp. 563–574.

Meadus R. (2000) Men in nursing: barriers to recruitment. *Nursing Forum* 35(3), 5–13.

Mericle B.P. (1983) The male as a psychiatric nurse. *Journal of Psychosocial Nursing and Mental Health Services* 21(11), 28–34.

Miers M. (2000) *Gender Issues and Nursing Practice*. Macmillan, London.

Morgan D. (1992) *Discovering Men*. Routledge, London.

Mosse G.L. (1996) *The Image of Man. The Creation of Modern Masculinity*. Oxford University Press, Oxford, UK.

Nordberg M. (2002) Constructing masculinity in women's worlds: men working as pre-school teachers and hairdressers. *NORA* 1(10), 26–37.

Okrainec G.D. (1994) Perceptions of nursing education held by male nursing students. *Western Journal of Nursing Research* 16(1), 94–107.

Parker I. (1992) *Discourse Dynamics: Critical Analysis for Social and Individual Psychology*. Routledge, London.

Phillips N. & Hardy C. (2002) *Discourse Analysis. Investigating Processes of Social Construction*. Sage, Thousand Oaks, CA.

Platzer H. (1993) Nursing care of gay and lesbian patients. *Nursing Standard* 7(17), 34–37.

Porter-O'Grady T. (2001) Beyond the walls: nursing in the entrepreneurial world. *Nursing Administration Quarterly* 25(2), 61–68.

Potter J. (1996) Discourse analysis and constructionist approaches: theoretical background. In *Handbook of Qualitative Research Methods for Psychology and the Social Sciences* (Richardson J.T.E., ed.), BPS Books, Leicester, UK, pp. 125–141.

Potter J. & Wetherell M. (1987) *Discourse and Social Psychology: Beyond Attitudes and Behaviour*. Sage, London.

Richmond J.P. & McKenna H. (1998) Homophobia: an evolutionary analysis of the concept as applied to nursing. *Journal of Advanced Nursing* 28(2), 362–369.

Romen P. & Anson O. (2005) Israeli men in nursing: social and personal motives. *Journal of Nursing Management* 13, 173-178.

Salvage J. (1985) *The Politics of Nursing*. William Heinemann Medical Books, London.

Sedgwick E.K. (1990) *Epistemology of the Closet*. University of California Press, Berkeley, CA.

Taylor I. & Robertson A. (1994) The health needs of gay men: a discussion of the literature and the implications for nursing. *Journal of Advanced Nursing* 20, 560–566.

Thompson M. (1987) *Gay Spirit: Myth and Meaning.* St Martin's, New York.

Tyson L. (1999) *Critical Theory Today. A User-Friendly Guide.* Garland Publishing, New York.

Weeks J. (1985) *Sexuality and its Discontents: Meanings, Myths and Modern Sexualities.* Routledge & Paul, London.

Williams C.L. (1989) *Gender Differences at Work: Women and Men in Nontraditional Occupations.* University of California Press, Los Angeles, CA.

Williams C.L. (1993) Introduction. In *Doing 'Women's Work'. Men in Nontraditional Occupations* (Williams C.L., ed), University of California Press, Berkeley, CA, pp. 1–9.

Williams C.L. (1995) *Still a Man's World. Men Who do Women's Work.* University of California Press, Berkeley, CA.

Wood L.A. & Kroger R.O. (2000) *Doing Discourse Analysis: Methods for Studying Action in Talk and Text.* Sage, Thousand Oaks, CA.

Periodical Bibliography

The following articles have been selected to supplement the diverse views presented in this chapter.

Nancy Baraza "Women Still Denied Equal Property Rights," *Daily Nation* (Nairobi), December 6, 2010.

Cherie Blair "Everyone Suffers When Women Bear the Brunt of Global Poverty," *Independent* (London), June 22, 2009.

John Carney and Lana Lam "Wan Chai Bars Shock Transgender Experts, Barring Them as 'Lady Boys,'" *South China Morning Post*, October 31, 2010.

Catherine Fox "Jobs for Women, but Not at the Top," *Australian Financial Review*, August 1, 2009.

Wallace Immen "How They Managed to Rise to the Top," *Globe and Mail* (Canada), November 13, 2009.

Alvine Kapitako "True Gender Equality Remains a Dream," *New Era* (Namibia), July 20, 2010.

Korea Times "Yawning Wage Gap," April 4, 2010.

Mercy Nalugo "Sex Workers Confront Ssekandi," *Monitor* (Uganda), December 15, 2010.

Kirsty Needham "All the Right Stuff, but Motherhood Needs Rule Teacher Out of Plum Job," *Sydney Morning Herald* (Australia), September 15, 2009.

Rita Trichur "Gays Still Fear Workplace Bias," *Toronto Star*, June 4, 2009.

William F. Vásquez "Ethnic and Gender Wage Discrimination in Guatemala," *Journal of Developing Areas*, vol. 44, no. 2, Spring 2011.

GLOBALVIEWPOINTS

CHAPTER 3

Racial and Ethnic Discrimination

In Ireland, People of African Descent Face Employment Discrimination

Edorodion Osa

In the following viewpoint, Dublin-based filmmaker and writer Edorodion Osa argues that people of African descent living in Ireland face discrimination in the workplace. He discusses a study recently published by the Economic and Social Research Institute (ESRI), an Irish think tank, that revealed that the employment outlook for people of African descent and other ethnic minorities has grown bleaker. Not only are they less likely to be hired, but ethnic minorities are also far less likely to be promoted than white candidates. Ultimately, Osa asserts, the Irish have to implement and enforce nondiscriminatory policies if Ireland is going to be competitive in the global marketplace.

As you read, consider the following questions:

1. How much more likely are people of African descent or other ethnic minorities to be unemployed than their white Irish counterparts?
2. According to the 2006 Irish census, what percentage of the nonwhite population is unemployed?
3. As explained by Osa, what is interculturalism?

Edorodion Osa, "Black Man's Burden in Ireland," *New African*, vol. 494, April 2010, pp. 96–98. Reproduced by permission.

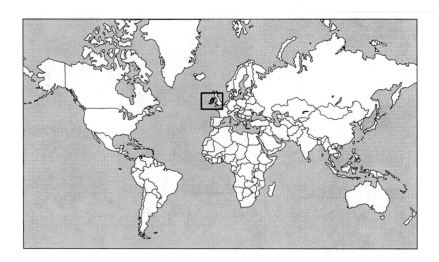

The Irish socioeconomic think tank, the Economic and Social Research Institute (ESRI), recently conducted a study on the experiences of black and other ethnic minority groups in the Irish labour market, with startling findings. Black people in Ireland are nine times more likely to be unemployed than their white Irish counterparts, apart from facing discrimination in access to employment.

It was a cold, wet and blustery morning at Dublin Airport and I had just arrived on an early bird flight from London Stansted. I produced a card from my wallet and dialled the telephone number on it. It was the telephone number of a cab company. Fifteen minutes later, a young man, probably in his early thirties, walked up to me and introduced himself as Thabo (not his real name), the taxi driver.

As we drove down the Mr, towards the M50, he told me he was originally from South Africa but had been settled in Ireland with his wife and children for the past two years. Thabo said he has a bachelor of engineering degree in electronics from a South African university but found it difficult to get a job as Irish employers did not like qualifications obtained in Africa.

He said he applied for several jobs without success, and in frustration, he had to go back to an Irish university to study for another degree in electronics engineering. He graduated two years ago but since then, his job-hunting story has remained the same.

Thabo's experience in the labour market is certainly a familiar ringtone in the ears of many black people in Ireland, a country where the culture of "doing things the Irish way" is deeply entrenched and where, until recently, the ethic of "doing business with your own kind" has never been problematic.

It also illustrates the enormity of the social barrier they face in their efforts to participate in the socioeconomic space of a society that has been moulded in the image of a nation of homogeneous white Catholics with a distinct cultural identity.

Black people in Ireland are less likely to secure high-level professional and managerial positions.

Among other findings of the ESRI's research, even when in employment, black people in Ireland are less likely to secure high-level professional and managerial positions, and are more likely to be abused in the workplace.

A separate piece of research carried out by WRC Consulting, a management consulting group, in collaboration with the Office of the Minister for Integration, reaffirmed the ESRI findings. The research revealed that while there is a high unemployment rate amongst other ethnic minority groups in relation to whites, black people are the most disproportionately unemployed in relation to all other ethnic groups, and are more likely to be found doing jobs that are below their qualification and skills levels. Furthermore, it found out that black people find public sector jobs particularly inaccessible and that Irish employers' practices tend to be racist towards them.

Over one-quarter of the black population in the country are unemployed, according to the 2006 census, the most recent head count in Ireland.

Eric Yao, the coordinator of the Africa Centre, a Dublin-based NGO which promotes the interests of people of African descent in Ireland, says the grim picture only reflected the plight of black people in the Celtic Tiger years when Ireland enjoyed unprecedented economic growth.

Now, Yao says, their situation is even more precarious as Irish employers use the current global recession to get rid of the few black people who were able to secure employment during the boom years.

"Black people have become the easy target. Africa Centre has been inundated with unemployed Africans looking for work. They are more likely to be the first to go when companies are shedding jobs as a result of the global credit crunch and they are more likely to suffer racism in the workplace than any other group."

"I remember one particular interview where I was asked 'why do you claim to be Irish when you are black?'"

Yao says that before he became the coordinator of the Africa Centre, he applied for several jobs without success. Originally from Ghana, he was initially prohibited from employment as he was a spouse of a non-EU doctor.

When the law was later amended to allow spouses of non-EU doctors access to employment, he did not even get short-listed for any interview despite having a master's degree in international relations and years of experience working at the United Nations.

"Irish employers look at your name and your nationality on your CV and when they are not Irish, you don't stand any chance," Yao says.

"When I got Irish citizenship, I changed my nationality, and because my name does not easily show me as an African, I got short-listed for many jobs within a short space of time. But when I appeared at the interviews, I drew reactions from people who were surprised at a black man claiming to be Irish.

"I remember one particular interview where I was asked 'why do you claim to be Irish when you are black?' There is discrimination in Ireland and the Irish are learning to live and deal with a large population of people of different ethnicities for the first time."

During the boom years, the Fianna Fáil Party led a coalition government that enunciated several integration policies based on "interculturalism", a concept predicated on the cross-fertilisation of the various cultures in Ireland and which encourages a two-way learning process between the dominant white-Irish culture and the emerging ethnic minority cultures.

Policies encouraging members of ethnic minorities to participate in the civic and democratic processes were put in place, while regulations to mainstream service delivery were also created.

Entry requirements into the police force were amended to attract people from ethnic minority backgrounds and local authorities were funded to initiate, support and encourage integration activities at local levels. Sports bodies were also given financial boosts in order to attract talented youth from black and ethnic minority backgrounds.

While John Curran, the minister charged with the responsibility of coordinating integration policies and programmes, was keen to enumerate these policy objectives and highlight their importance, at the last annual general meeting of the European Jesuit Refugee Service, some ethnic minority-led organisations cast doubts over government's commitment to implementing them. They also question the political will to economically empower blacks and other ethnic minority groups.

"Those policies were formulated without due consultations with ethnic minority oganisations," says Yao. "Some time ago, I was invited to an anti-racism ceremony and I was presented with a policy document. My first question was 'what was the input of members of ethnic minorities into this policy document?' They could not provide any answer. The government is now focused on steering the economy out of recession so integration and ethnic empowerment have been relegated to the back burner."

He says that as one way of stemming black unemployment, the Africa Centre has designed a training programme to assist black people who have lost their jobs and those who have been unemployed long term to set up their own businesses.

"We get them together; look at their CVs and their educational qualifications and skills," says Yao. "We then identify those with the necessary skills and business ideas and we link them to where they can get financial support and help on how to manage their businesses. We have already had the first session and we are now preparing for the next one to be held soon."

Attempts to find out the government's plan to address the disproportionately high rate of black unemployment from Curran were unsuccessful. Instead, he said issues relating to employment should be addressed to the Department of Enterprise, Trade and Innovation, a department which does not have jurisdiction over people settled in Ireland but which only has the remit to issue work permits to non-EEA citizens wishing to work in the country.

However, Mary Corcoran, a migration expert and professor of urban sociology at the National University of Ireland, Maynooth, says access to opportunity structures should be made available to all on an equal basis regardless of ethnicity and that includes access to meaningful employment opportunities for blacks.

"If Ireland is to thrive in a globalised economy, it has to learn to deal with the 'other' and move beyond blatant racism," she says, "Irish people are extremely ethnocentric and are not open to difference and this prejudicial behaviour is also reflected in the reluctance of employers to engage with blacks in the labour market."

She says there is tremendous racialisation of economic opportunities and employers always advantage white over black candidates in the labour market.

Black people, she points out, are the most disadvantaged because they are seen as the most different and their names are always a signifier for Irish employers to discriminate against them.

Corcoran says the economic recession has further reinforced the "other" by creating a "drawbridge mentality" where the Irish have become increasingly concerned about "our own". "Our own," she stresses, "becomes increasingly narrowly defined as white vs. others, but they have to learn how to be colour-blind when dealing with people and that includes Irish employers. Ireland should also avoid the pitfall of creating neighbourhoods along the lines of ethnicity and social class. For example, it should not make social housing exclusively for blacks and other ethnic minorities as that could lead to social stigmatisation."

Black people . . . are seen as the most different and their names are always a signifier for Irish employers to discriminate against them.

While it is obvious that there are policies and legislation put in place to address economic and social inequalities in Ireland, there seems to be no urgency to implement them soon. In the words of Corcoran: "The Irish have to quickly learn how not to marginalise people of colour and migrants in order to avoid potential social problems in the future."

In South Africa, Race No Longer Affects Economic Status

Jeremy Seekings

Jeremy Seekings is a professor of political studies and sociology at the University of Cape Town and the author of many books, including Class, Race, and Inequality in South Africa. *In the following viewpoint, he argues that race remains an important part of South African culture, but it no longer limits nonwhite persons economically. He asserts that attitudes about ethnicity have changed since the end of apartheid and that there are now some advantages to being black-skinned. In his view, race has become less of a source of discrimination than class.*

As you read, consider the following questions:

1. Explain the "dictator game" in the experiment carried out by Justine Burns.
2. What was the most significant finding of the 2003 countrywide South African study?
3. What percentage of all African graduates obtain their first job in the public sector?

In a world in which racial labelling and discrimination are regrettably commonplace, the South African system of apartheid stood out as an extreme attempt to order a society

Jeremy Seekings, "The Continuing Salience of Race: Discrimination and Diversity in South Africa," *Journal of Contemporary African Studies*, vol. 26, no. 1, January 2008, pp. 1–2, 16–23. Reprinted by permission of the publisher Taylor & Francis Ltd., http://www.informaworld.com.

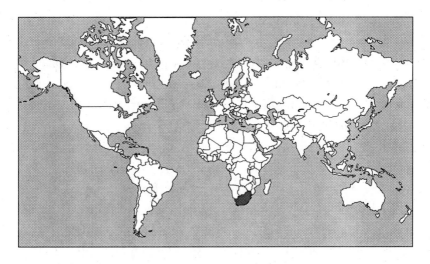

explicitly and systematically according to racial categories. Many aspects of apartheid were not unique to South Africa. In the aftermath of slavery, colonial (and especially settler) societies in Africa generally practised racial segregation. In the USA and Brazil, most black people were denied the vote through literacy and other qualifications (until the 1960s in the USA, and as late as the 1980s in Brazil). In much of Latin America and the Caribbean, as well as the southern states of the USA, white people owned the land whilst landless black people worked for them. Racism and racial discrimination have been almost universal in the twentieth century. The concept of 'apartheid' has even been applied to cities in the USA in the late twentieth century. Indeed, apartheid—as implemented by the National Party government in power from 1948 to 1994—was built on the foundations of racialised colonial and settler societies in which a minority of white settlers—farmers and workers—lived amidst an indigenous or 'native' majority. What made apartheid unique was its systematic depth and breadth, as the powers of a modern state were deployed to order society along 'racial' lines, going far beyond racism and racial discrimination to generalised social engineering around state-sanctioned racial ideology and legislation.

It would be astonishing if post-apartheid South African society was not shaped profoundly by the experience of apartheid, remaining distinctive in terms of the social, political or economic roles played by 'race'. Despite the rhetorical commitment to non-racialism of the major 'liberation movement' (the African National Congress [ANC]), together with its allies inside the country, during the struggle against apartheid, and despite the abolition of apartheid-era racial legislation and the adoption of a widely lauded constitution, race does indeed remain ever present in contemporary South Africa. To a large extent this is due to a deep-rooted and enduring consciousness of race in society. To some extent it is due to factors that reflect choices made by post-apartheid political elites: the use of the race card in public life, including in politics, and new policies of racial discrimination involving, especially, affirmative action in employment, with the stated objective of redressing the disadvantages experienced by non-white South Africans (either collectively or individually) under apartheid.

Racial discrimination in economic life against black people has been largely ended in South Africa. Some lingering discrimination by white employers against black people no doubt persists, but it is probably more than offset by the effects of affirmative action. Persistent racial inequalities reflect class stratification rather than racial discrimination, as we have argued at length elsewhere (Seekings and Nattrass 2005). Income is distributed within the African population almost as unequally as within the population as a whole, as opportunities have expanded rapidly for many African people to move into better-paid occupations at the same time as many others languish in poverty because of poor schooling and chronic unemployment. Citizenship—whether civil, political or social—is no longer defined in racial terms. Yet society remains highly racialised. Inter-racial contact, yet alone marriage, remains very limited.

This continuing salience of race is surprising in several respects. First, the deracialisation of citizenship and public policy (with the minor exception of 'affirmative action' and 'black economic empowerment') has removed the impetus to racial identities that many scholars emphasise when discussing the South African past (for example, MacDonald 2006). Secondly, the precise salience of race in South Africa stands in sharp contrast to other societies with which South Africa is often and usefully compared. Telles (2005) shows how important race is in contemporary Brazil, but in *some* rather than all respects. Contrary to the Brazilian ideology of 'racial democracy', racial discrimination seems significant in economic life. Yet, in terms of identities and social interactions, Brazilians are remarkably non-racial. Telles distinguishes between vertical relationships, in which race is important, and horizontal ones, in which it is not. Post-apartheid South Africa appears to be the opposite of this. The vertical dimension of racism appears to have been largely eliminated (or perhaps even reversed), but the horizontal dimension appears resilient (or perhaps has even increased, as racial differences within the increasingly multiracial middle class have grown and become more visible). . . .

Racial discrimination in economic life against black people has been largely ended in South Africa.

Discriminatory Attitudes and Experiences

Ethnographic research in neighbourhoods and schools suggests that racial differences and divisions remain pronounced, but finds little evidence of the kind of brutal racism associated with white South Africans in the early apartheid period. Experimental research on behaviour and survey-based research on attitudes supports this assessment. Experimental research on race has been pioneered in South Africa by Justine Burns. In one of Burns' experiments, secondary school students in Cape Town played the 'dictator game', in which players are given money and then choose how much to pass onto anonymous 'partners', whose photo they have seen but otherwise know nothing about. Using a photo allowed Burns to test for the effect of the partners' race, or at least race in terms of physical appearance. Burns found that there was no direct race effect, that is, that players did not discriminate against partners who appeared to be racially different. This behaviour appeared to be motivated by an aversion to inherited inequality, and racial appearance was taken as a proxy for inherited inequality (Burns 2004). In more complex 'trust games', students exhibited complex patterns of racial interaction—but for the most part did not exhibit the 'ingroup' bias that might be expected (Burns 2006).

The participants in Burns' experiments know that they are in an experiment, and this might affect their behaviour. The participants do not know, however, that inter-racial interaction is the focus of the research. In surveys, respondents might also select responses in the knowledge that they are being researched, but the use of 'vignettes' can help to disguise the focus of the research. Respondents are presented with one or more vignettes describing a situation, followed by a question or series of questions related to the situation. Sniderman and Piazza (1993) used vignettes to examine 'modern' forms of racism in the USA. In their 'laid-off worker' vignette, respondents were presented with a scenario in which a person (or subject) is retrenched, and are then invited to suggest how much (if any) financial assistance that person should receive from the government whilst looking for work. The scenario varies insofar as the subject (or retrenched person) is given different characteristics: white or black, male or female, younger or older, single or married, with or without children, and dependable or not dependable. The 2003 Cape Area Study, conducted with a small sample in Cape Town, employed a variant of the 'laid-off worker' vignette to probe the effects of race on perceptions of distributive justice. By including a range of characteristics for each subject, the respondent's attention is being diverted in part at least from the racial characteristic.

Questions about distributive justice are a telling test of one dimension of racial attitudes because the official ideology of apartheid emphasised that each racial group (and each ethnic group within the African population) should look after its own: white South Africans were not responsible for the poverty of black South Africans; rich South Africans were only responsible for poor South Africans if they were members of the same racially demarcated 'community'. One might expect that the overriding racialisation of society under apartheid and the continuing salience of race have resulted in a close correlation between race and attitudes toward distribution or distributive justice. The government, the ANC and the media frequently accuse white South Africans of being opposed to 'transformation', that is, to redistributive social and economic policies. If this was the case, then we would expect to find that South Africans will assess what other members of their own racial group (that is, 'insiders') deserve more favourably or positively than that of members of other racial groups (that is, 'outsiders').

Ethnographic research . . . finds little evidence of the kind of brutal racism associated with white South Africans in the early apartheid era.

The results of the 'laid-off worker' experiment in Cape Town in 2003 suggested that the race of the respondent and the race of the subject were of little import in whether a respondent considered a subject deserving. For example, white respondents did *not* discriminate significantly against African or coloured subjects. But there were clear (and counterintuitive) race effects on the amount that the respondent said that the subject should receive per month from the government. White respondents were more generous, perhaps because they had a more inflated view of what constituted a 'minimum' income; more curiously, black and coloured respondents as well as white respondents suggested that larger grants be made to white than to African or coloured subjects (Seekings forthcoming)!

The 2005 Cape Area Study extended this vignette (as well as asking several other vignette-style questions), with a larger sample, but also confined to Cape Town. Instead of asking about the scenario of a retrenched worker, respondents in 2005 were presented with a wider range of circumstances in which a subject might be considered deserving of financial assistance. Respondents were first told that 'The government provides grants to some people in need, for example old-age pensions to elderly people. I am going to describe a situation, and then ask you what the government should do to help the person involved.' A specific subject was then described. The subjects varied between interviews. Firstly, the general circumstances of the subject varied. Some subjects were described as retrenched workers, others as people who were sick; some were disabled and others abandoned by husbands; and so on. A range of other social and demographic characteristics—including race—were varied also. The 2005 data showed most of the same patterns as the 2003 data: the race of the subject made little or no difference, white respondents were a little less positive in their initial assessment of desert, but a lot more generous in the sums they 'awarded'. Unlike 2003, there was no indication that respondents were more generous to white subjects. In this dimension of social attitudes, race plays little effect, and there is little or no evidence of racism or racial discrimination (Seekings 2007). These findings from survey vignettes are not dissimilar to Burns' findings using data from field experiments.

White South Africans have no qualms, however, in expressing opposition to race-based policies, such as affirmative action and black economic empowerment. Several studies suggest that there is wide and strong support for government interventions to help the poor, but only among African people is there a majority in favour of race-based affirmative action (in employment), black economic empowerment or redistribution of land (ILO 2004; Roberts 2006).

Survey data suggest that most South Africans believe that 'race relations' have improved since the end of apartheid, and neither surveys nor field experiments provide evidence of significant racial discrimination in attitudes or experimental behaviour. But discrimination might persist in other domains, and it is even more likely that discrimination is *perceived* as continuing.

A larger minority of white and Indian people report experiencing discrimination than among African or coloured people.

The 2005 Cape Area Study asked about recent experiences of discrimination. Respondents were asked whether, in the five years since 2000, they had 'been treated worse than other people or benefited' because of their race. Very few respondents said that they had experienced negative racial discrimination. Most African respondents said that they had benefited because they were black, whilst most coloured and white respondents said that they had neither benefited not been treated worse.

This was followed by a series of questions about experiences in specific settings (*see* Figure 3 [adapted]). Almost all African respondents reported that they had been watched or followed in shops, compared to a minority of coloured respondents and very few white respondents. Larger proportions of African respondents than coloured or white respondents reported experiencing each of the other four situations (being treated with less respect, being treated worse in restaurants and shops, being treated by people as if they were afraid of you, and being treated by other people as if they were better than you). But in these other four situations the proportions of African, coloured and white respondents who reported that they had had the experience were not massively different. For example, just over one-half of African respondents reported being treated with less respect, compared to over one-third of coloured and white respondents.

These results are broadly consistent with the findings of countrywide data from 2003. Most South Africans reported that they never feel that they are being discriminated against. A larger minority of white and Indian people report experiencing discrimination than among African or coloured people. Discrimination is perceived as occurring primarily at work (especially by African people), when applying for jobs (especially among white and coloured people), and in shops (especially among white people, curiously) (Roefs 2006, 88–9).

Discrimination and Disadvantage

The effects of race in the labour market were much studied in the early 1990s. From the 1920s to the 1970s, racial discrimination generally confined African people to low-paid occupations. When African and white people were in the same occupation—for example, teaching and the police—white employees were paid more than their African counterparts. But this picture began to change dramatically from the 1970s. Crankshaw (1997) demonstrated the steady, and at times rapid, rise of African workers into better-paid occupations in the later apartheid period. Moll (2000) showed that the share of inequality in the distribution of wages that was accounted for by inter-racial differences declined from 65% in 1980 to 42% in 1993, whilst the share accounted for by intra-racial differences rose from 35 to 58%. The racial wage gap declined

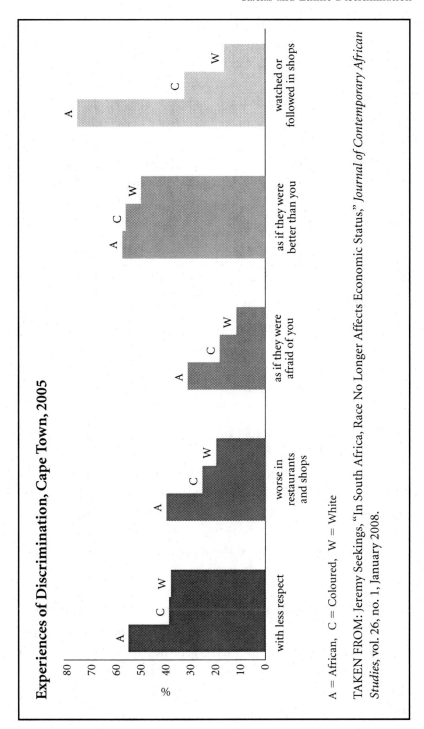

Experiences of Discrimination, Cape Town, 2005

A = African, C = Coloured, W = White

TAKEN FROM: Jeremy Seekings, "In South Africa, Race No Longer Affects Economic Status," *Journal of Contemporary African Studies*, vol. 26, no. 1, January 2008.

but still remained large, with median earnings for African workers only about one-quarter of the median for white workers, in 1995 (Bhorat and Leibbrandt 2001, 83; see also Burger and Woolard 2005, 19). But a series of studies demonstrated that this persistent racial wage gap was due primarily to differences in education, skill, location (urban/rural), and economic sector, rather than by racial discrimination per se. Moll also found that racial discrimination amounted to 20% of mean African wage in 1980 but just 12% in 1993. Whilst several other studies used data from the mid-1990s to re-examine racial wage discrimination, there has been a dearth of studies using post-1995 data. Several recent studies of the labour market pay no attention at all to racial discrimination, focusing instead on the unambiguously pressing topic of unemployment and job creation (for example, Burger and Woolard 2005; Oosthuizen 2006).

There has also been a dramatic shrinkage in the racial wage gap among managers.

There appears to be just one study of racial discrimination using post-1995 data. Burger and Jafta (2006) use a set of decomposition techniques on data from October Household Surveys (OHSs) and Labour Force Surveys (LFSs) between 1995 and 2004 to assess changes over time in the 'unexplained' part of the racial gap in both racial employment and (formal sector) wage gaps—with 'unexplained' meaning unexplained by other readily measured variables such as years of schooling and location. They find that there has been a narrowing of the racial wage gap since 1994 at the top end of the wage distribution, but not overall. The unexplained element remains, that is, being white apparently continues to earn a premium in the labour market, essentially because white people earn higher returns on their education than do Indian, coloured or, especially, African people.

As most of these econometric studies emphasise, returns to education surely continue to vary by race because of the enormous but unmeasured differences in the quality of education, combined with the similarly unmeasured benefits that social capital bring to young people from middle-class backgrounds. Taking such factors into account would surely reduce considerably the 'unexplained' component of the racial wage gap, and reduce further the importance of racial discrimination relative to other factors such as inequalities in real skills and useful contacts.

Burger and Jafta's work points to the importance of distinguishing between different sections of the labour market. Unlike in (say) Brazil or the USA, there are few unskilled white workers competing with black workers for low-paid employment (and of the small number of unskilled white workers, some might have hidden class advantages, for example young people with part-time jobs as waitresses). It is at the top end of the labour market that the effects of persistent racial discrimination against African people or affirmative action in their benefit would be concentrated. There are unfortunately few studies of the top end of the labour market, especially among young entrants. But some data suggests that, in some sectors, patterns of discrimination have changed markedly over very short periods of time. In the late 1990s, the public sector was the primary venue for affirmative action. The proportion of public sector managers who were African rose from 30% in 1995 to 51% in 2001. The proportion of senior managers who were African rose from 33 to 43% (Thompson and Woolard 2002). As many as 70% of all African graduates obtain their first job in the public sector (cited in Altman 2006, 69). In the early 2000s, legislation has pushed larger private sector employers to similar shifts in employment patterns. There has also been a dramatic shrinkage in the racial wage gap among managers (cited in Altman 2006).

A second, complicating factor in the analysis of racial discrimination in labour market outcomes (that is, employment and wages) using cross-sectional data is that substantial numbers of younger white people have emigrated, or are at least outside of the country for long periods of time. Whilst they might be outside the South African labour market, their choice is probably not entirely exogenous to conditions in the labour market. I am unaware of any studies that examine the real effects of affirmative action legislation on the labour market for school-leavers or, especially, university graduates, but there is no shortage of anecdotal evidence that young white men and women *believe* that affirmative action policies and practices are foreclosing opportunities for employment, and that this perception influences decisions about emigration. If it was true that white graduates are emigrating to avoid unemployment (perhaps because they would 'choose' unemployment over employment in occupations that are inferior to those to which they aspired), then emigration would cause analyses of cross-sectional data to *under*-estimate the effects of affirmative action.

Unfortunately there is no experimental research in South Africa assessing the extent and patterns of racial (or other) discrimination in the labour market. If such research was conducted, however, it is likely that it would find that in occupations in which there are applicants from all racial groups (that is, excluding unskilled employment), modest racial discrimination is practised in favour of black applicants through affirmative action and black economic empowerment.

Panel studies offer a promising way forward for the empirical analysis of patterns and dynamics of advantage and disadvantage in post-apartheid South Africa. One such study is the Cape Area Panel Study (CAPS), which interviewed a representative sample of almost 5000 young people (aged between 14 and 22) in 2002, and has since re-interviewed this panel three times (in 2003–04, 2005, and 2006) (see Lam et al.

2005). CAPS has collected detailed data on schooling and entry into the labour market, as well as on sexual and reproductive health and experiences within families and households. Most data are collected from the young people themselves, but data are also collected from parents and other older household members, and data on individuals and households have been combined with community- and school-level data. The problem with panel studies is that data collection and cleaning are so time consuming that there are inevitable delays before panel data are available for analysis and longer delays before analyses are completed. A second problem is that attrition results in incomplete data. Given the difficulties of collecting data from or on emigrants, it is likely that CAPS will be able to offer only a partial picture of how and why and with what consequences young people enter the labour market. The South African Human Sciences Research Council is also conducting panel studies among cohorts of matriculants (that is, students writing the grade 12 examination) and university graduates, which will provide a fuller picture of what is happening at the top end of the labour market.

It is likely, however, that panel studies will confirm the following. Most children from poor neighbourhoods—almost all of whom are African—grow up in home environments that are unconducive to educational success, and attend schools where the quality of education is very poor. Many remain in school until their late teens, but are unable to acquire many skills. Their ability to find employment is constrained by their lack of skills and experience, their location far from most job opportunities, and their lack of the right contacts, i.e., people who have jobs and can therefore help them to find employment. Many move into the underclass of chronically unemployed, with intermittent short spells of unskilled work. On the other hand, children from middle-class neighbourhoods— who comprise rapidly rising numbers of African as well as Indian and white children—attend better schools, enjoy the benefits of middle-class home environments, and gain work experience through part-time jobs (especially in school holidays). They move into higher education and then into the labour market. White middle-class children enjoy the relative benefits of wider and deeper social networks, but the disadvantage of being white in an affirmative action environment.

Race remains relevant in South Africa for primarily cultural reasons.

Conclusion

The available evidence suggests that race remains of enormous social and cultural importance despite a decline in economic—and political—importance. Earnings and incomes reflect race far less than class. This raises questions, however, about the meaning of class in the South African context. In its intellectual seedbed in northwest Europe during the industrial revolution, there was generally a close relationship between 'objective' class positions (in terms of relationships to the means of production) and everyday cultures. As E.P. Thompson [a British historian] argued famously, the working class was made not only by the changing form and shape of industrial capitalism but also cultural struggles of dominant and subordinate classes. In South Africa, 'race'—understood as a social and cultural phenomenon, not biologically—has shaped profoundly cultural change, interacting complexly with the growth of modern state and a capitalist economy. Whilst the social question predominated in Britain and most of northwestern Europe, the national question retains an everyday salience in South Africa.

Insofar as this is the case, then South Africa would appear to be the opposite to Brazil, where race is of limited cultural and even social importance but of continuing economic significance. In the terms used by Telles, in Brazil there is racism in terms of vertical relations but not of horizontal relations, whilst in South Africa there is 'racism'—or at least the acknowledgement of racial difference—in terms of horizontal relations but not of vertical relations. In Brazil, inter-racial marriage and racial discrimination in employment are both common. In South Africa, after apartheid (and subject to caution with respect to the extent and effect of affirmative action), neither is common.

Race remains relevant in South Africa for primarily cultural reasons. Most South Africans have clear racial identities (although they might not be their most important identities) and readily view others in racial terms (although not only in such terms). This is not simply a lingering manifestation of racism. Indeed, experimental and other research suggests remarkably little racism in terms of racial discrimination in assessments of (for example) trustworthiness or desert. Rather, it reflects the persistence of racial discrimination in a softer sense, that is, in terms of social preferences. South Africans may not be hostile to racialised others, but prefer to live and generally socialise with culturally similar neighbours, and for their kin to marry within racial (that is, cultural) groups rather than outside them.

But the available evidence on post-apartheid South Africa is sadly limited. Little progress has been made yet with respect to two key kinds of study. First, data from panel studies are yet to be used to explore precisely how and why 'race' shapes progress through school and into the labour market. Secondly, there are still too few ethnographic studies of how 'race', 'class' and (especially) cultures are made and understood in the lived experience of South Africans, at home, in neighbourhoods, in schools and in workplaces. In South Africa, as in Brazil, we are only beginning to unravel the complicated interactions of race, class and culture in the contemporary context.

References

Altman, M. 2006. Wage Determination in South Africa: What do we know? *Transformation* 60: 58–89.

Bhorat, H., and M. Leibbrandt. 2001. Correlates of vulnerability in the South African labour market. In *Fighting Poverty: Labour Markets and Inequality in South Africa*, eds. H. Bhorat, M. Leibbrandt, M. Maziya, S. Van der Berg and I. Woolard. Cape Town: University of Cape Town Press.

Burger R., and R. Jafta. 2006. Returns to race: Labour market discrimination in post-apartheid South Africa. Stellenbosch Economic Working Paper 04/06, University of Stellenbosch.

Burger, R., and I. Woolard. 2005. The state of the labour market in South Africa after the first decade of democracy. Centre for Social Science Research Working paper 133, University of Cape Town.

Burns, J. 2004. Inequality aversion and group identity in a segmented society. Unpublished paper, University of cape Town.

————. 2006. Racial stereotypes, stigma and trust in post-apartheid South Africa. *Economic Modelling* 23: 805–21.

Crankshaw, O. 1997. *Race, class and the changing division of labour under apartheid*. London: Routledge.

International Labour Office (ILO). 2004. *Economic security for a better world*. Geneva: ILO.

Lam, D., J. Seekings, et al. 2005. *The Cape Area Panel Study (CAPS): An introduction and user's guide*. Cape Town: Centre for Social Science Research, University of Cape Town.

MacDonald, M. 2006. *Why race matters in South Africa*. Cambridge, MA: Harvard University Press.

Moll, P. 2000. Discrimination is declining in South Africa but inequality is not. *Journal for Studies in Economics and Econometrics* 24, no. 3: 91–108.

Oosthuizen, M. 2006. The post-apartheid labour market: 1995–2004. DPRU Working Paper 06/103, Development Policy Research Unit, University of Cape Town.

Roberts, B. 2006. The happy transition? Attitudes to poverty and inequality after a decade of democracy. In *South African social attitudes: Changing times, diverse voices*, eds. U. Pillay, B. Roberts and S. Rule, 101–30. Cape Town: HSRC Press.

Roefs, M. 2006. Identity and race relations. In *South African social attitudes: Changing times, diverse voices*, eds. U. Pillay, B. Roberts and S. Rule, 77–97. Cape Town: HSRC Press.

Seekings, J. 2007. Racial and class discrimination. In assessments of 'Just desert' in post-apartheid Cape Town. Unpublished paper, University of Cape Town.

Seekings, J., and N. Nattrass. 2005. *Class, race and inequality in South Africa*. New Haven, CT: Yale University Press.

Sniderman, P., and T. Piazza. 1993. *The scar of race*. Cambridge, MA: Belknap Press.

Telles, E. 2005. *Race in another America: The significance of skin color in Brazil*. Princeton, NJ: Princeton University Press.

Thompson, K., and I. Woolard. 2002. Achieving employment equity in the public service: A study of changes between 1995 and 2001. DPRU Working Paper 02/61, Development Policy Research Unit, University of Cape Town.

Germany's Discrimination of Roma Continues

Martin Kriekenbaum

Martin Kriekenbaum is a regular contributor to the World Socialist Web Site, which is published by leadership of the world socialist movement. In the following viewpoint, Kriekenbaum argues that the Roma people continue to be targets of discrimination in Germany. They are not given access to social programs, and they are routinely deported without due process. He also notes that Roma children are denied the opportunity to regularly attend school and very few Roma adults are gainfully employed. Unfortunately, the situation for Roma is not isolated to Germany but persists across much of Europe.

As you read, consider the following questions:

1. To what country is the German government deporting the Roma?
2. Approximately how many Roma sought refuge in Germany from the war in Yugoslavia in the 1990s?
3. When did the Roma arrive in Germany?

At a press conference directly after the EU (European Union) summit in Brussels two weeks ago [September 2010], the French President Nicolas Sarkozy caused a diplomatic storm, when he stated that German Chancellor Angela

Martin Kriekenbaum, "Poverty, Segregation and Discrimination for the Roma in Germany," World Socialist Web Site, October 2, 2010. Reprinted by permission.

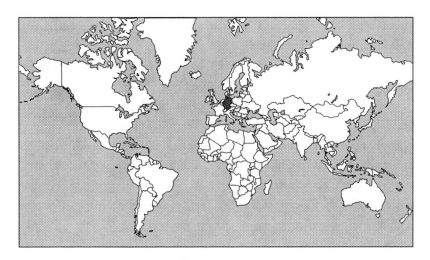

Merkel had signalled to him "her intention to have (Roma) camps cleared away in the coming weeks". His statement was immediately denied by the German government, which justified its claim principally by asserting there were no Roma camps to be found anywhere in Germany.

Politicians from German opposition parties also sprang to the chancellor's aid, levelling sharp criticism at Sarkozy. Olaf Scholz (SPD—Social Democratic Party) accused the French president of wanting to distract the people from his domestic political problems. Gregor Gysi (Left Party) even presumed that, "she (Merkel) couldn't have uttered such nonsense, because we don't have those kinds of camps in Germany".

There are indeed no camps in Germany comparable to those in France. Authorities immediately dispersed makeshift settlements in Berlin and Frankfurt when desperate Roma[1] from Bulgaria and Romania had set up camps there out in the open. Nevertheless, the German government is planning the deportation of Roma on a massive scale—but to Kosovo rather than Romania. The inhumanity of such an undertaking on

1. Romas are an ethnic group with origin in South Asia who are located throughout Europe.

the part of the German authorities is hardly less alarming than that of the French government. This is especially so because the Roma, together with the Jews, were the principal targets of the Nazi genocide.

On April 14, [2010] Interior Minister Thomas de Maizière (CDU—Christian Democratic Union) signed an agreement with his Kosovan counterparts, obliging Kosovo to take 14,000 refugees. About 10,000 of these will be Roma, who had fled during the German-backed war in former Yugoslavia. At the time, NATO's [North Atlantic Treaty Organization's] Kosovo militia allies expelled more than two-thirds of the 150,000 Roma from Kosovo.

The Roma, together with the Jews, were the principal targets of the Nazi genocide.

They will now be forced to return, although they have no chance of making a viable life in Kosovo. Investigations, carried out in the country by political scientist Peter Widmann, show that unemployment among Roma in Kosovo is almost 100 percent, and Roma families are commonly segregated. Particularly hard-hit are the 2,000 Roma children the German government wants to deport. Some of them were born in Germany and cannot speak a word of Albanian. According to Widmann, three-quarters of the children of deported refugees in Kosovo do not attend school.

Nevertheless, the German government insists that conditions for Roma in Kosovo have improved in recent years. In the view of the Federal Ministry of the Interior, there exists no "imminent danger, arising solely from membership to a particular ethnic group", and it is also alleged that "economic and social conditions in the state, targeted to take in deportees" are irrelevant for the deportation process. According to UNICEF (United Nations Children's Fund), however, the deportation procedures violate in practice the United Nations

Convention on the Rights of the Child because of their failure to ensure maintenance of a humane existence.

Responding to an enquiry from the Left Party, the German Interior Ministry recently confirmed that it would be adhering to its deportation plans that were first reported a year ago by the *Süddeutsche Zeitung* newspaper. It can thus be assumed that Sarkozy did not simply invent Merkel's comment about the clearance of camps, but had been informed of the forthcoming deportation of Roma.

Harassment of Refugees

The harassment of Roma in Germany is not restricted to those soon to be deported. Roma, who are allowed to stay in the country on sufferance, who possess German citizenship and whose families have lived in Germany for generations, are also facing social discrimination.

A total of about 50,000 Roma sought refuge in Germany from the war in Yugoslavia in the 1990s. More than two-thirds of them have not been recognized as refugees—that is, they have been denied a secure right of stay and are only there on sufferance, pending further developments. This temporary right of residence is issued and reissued for only short periods of time, normally no longer than 6 months, so that refugees face the possibility of being deported at any time.

In line with this kind of temporary resident status, access to almost all the state's social benefits is excluded. They have no right to participate in integration programs and language courses, and they are not allowed to travel outside the municipality or administrative district assigned to them. Offences against these restrictions on freedom of movement incur harsh punishments.

Because they are refugees, moreover, the law covering social provision for asylum seekers allows them only a reduced amount of social support. Single parents thus receive only about €230 a month and other household members only

€200. However, municipal authorities often only pay out the legally specified minimum amount of €40 in cash, and provide the rest in the form of essential, tangible goods. These refugees also have no claim to child or parental allowances, and are not medically insured, receiving only emergency medical care.

In line with this kind of temporary resident status, access to almost all the state's social benefits is excluded.

To deter future refugees' claims, they are assigned to hostels and provisional housing, lying on the outer limits of towns or industrial estates. So-called "container detention stations" are set up for Roma in some municipalities—a ship for the accommodation of 200 refugees was used in Hamburg's harbour. Otherwise, old school buildings, shabby hotels and administrative sites serve as refugee hostels, all characterised by poor structural conditions, deficiencies in basic equipment and absence of social care.

Although some municipalities have begun to provide Roma with rented flats, the accommodation predicament of the vast majority of refugees has scarcely changed.

Challenges for Roma Children

As refugees, Roma are also subject to a restriction on gaining employment or taking part in training programs and further education. Consequently, bleak prospects are assured, especially for young Roma. Particularly affected in this respect are the children, who are refused the right to attend school in federal states such as Hesse and Saarland.

Yet it is often the case that even those children who can attend school fail to receive a decent education. The authorities then put this down to "cultural specifics" relating to Roma, who are disparaged for "not being interested in school" and being "non-conformist". The reasons for this are to be found in the children's living conditions, which are determined by the state authorities themselves.

Discrimination in the education system and on the labour and housing markets drives many Roma into social isolation.

The reallocation and closure of refugee hostels continually forces the Roma in and out of various places of accommodation. For children, this often involves a change in school and a renewed effort to integrate. De-registrations and failure to re-register then lead to irregular school attendance and missed lessons.

However, parents—for whom there are no language courses, and who are often poorly educated or have never attended school themselves—are sweepingly reproached for not looking after their children. As a result, the children of Roma refugees are considered unwilling to learn and referred, without any diagnostic testing, to special schools, where they are in effect denied any chance of job training.

Discrimination in the education system and on the labour and housing markets drives many Roma into social isolation. Negative experiences with official authorities also lead to distrust and alienation. This in turn is cited by right-wing demagogues as proof that Sinti and Roma are "incapable of integration".

Persecution of Sinti and Roma

In addition to refugees from Eastern Europe, there are also Sinti[2] and Roma people in Germany, who have lived there for generations, most possessing German citizenship. According to the EU's Charter of Fundamental Rights and the European Commission's Framework Convention for the Protection of

2. Also thought to be of South Asian origins, the Sinti are Romas who arrived in Germany in the Middle Ages.

National Minorities, Sinti and Roma are recognised as a minority people and entitled to special rights and protection.

It is therefore surprising how little is known about their social situation. This is firstly evident in relation to the size of this population group. As only the citizenship and not the ethnicity of members of the population is recorded, the number of Sinti and Roma with German passports can only be roughly estimated. This number is usually assumed to be some 70,000 people. Added to this, must be the approximately 50,000 refugees from former Yugoslavia and Kosovo, among who are about 20,000 children. However, there are also estimations claiming 200,000 Roma in Germany.

Sinti and Roma certainly do not belong to one ethnically homogeneous group. They have very different histories of settlement and speak different languages. The Sinti arrived in Germany about 600 years ago, and the Roma in the nineteenth century. What they have in common, however, is a history plagued with discrimination.

After the foundation of the German national state in 1871 and the consequent expansion of the administrative system, persecution of minorities increased. A special squad, the so-called "Gypsy Central [Office]", was set up in Munich in 1899. Officially named "Central Office for the Fight Against the Gypsy Nuisance", its jurisdiction was extended to cover the whole of the German empire in 1929. The main task of this branch of the police force was to compile a systematic register of the Sinti and Roma—an operation the Nazi regime was able to extend in order to build its racial segregation and extermination programs.

Directly after [Adolf] Hitler came to power, the Nazis set up "gypsy camps" in towns and cities, and released the "Circular Decree for the Combat of the Gypsy Plague". From 1942, they began programmed mass deportations to the extermination camps of Auschwitz and Birkenau, where 500,000 Sinti and Roma from throughout Europe were murdered. From the approximately 25,000 Sinti and Roma still living in Germany at the start of the Second World War, more than 15,000 were killed by the Nazi terror regime.

What they have in common, however, is a history plagued with discrimination.

However, the persecution and murder of Sinti and Roma was hushed up and denied for decades after the war. Occasionally, authorities even continued the Nazis' inhumane policies. In Bavaria in 1953, the "Vagrants Central" was established as a direct successor to the "Gypsy Central". It was led by Josef Eichberger, who had formerly been in charge of the Reich Central Exchange for the Deportation of Sinti and Roma. The Vagrants Central customarily drew on old Nazi files. Numerous Sinti and Roma, who had become stateless under the Nazi regime, had to wait until the 1980s before they were again granted German citizenship.

The German authorities also continued the ideology of persecution employed in the Nazi regime. They alleged that all Sinti and Roma were incapable of integration, owing to their race and culture; that they were driven by a roving instinct; and that they had criminal tendencies.

Although the Sinti and Roma were generally pressured to remain in one spot, respective municipal authorities tried to prevent settlements within their own administrative districts. Alternately victims of ghettoisation and eviction, the survivors of the concentration camps were only granted caravan parking space without any water or electricity facilities by some of the municipalities; elsewhere they were allocated to low-grade residential areas in remote places.

Settled, but Destitute

In spite of this, the great majority of Sinti and Roma have long become settled. However, only a small proportion of them have been able to raise their standard of living. The deplorable social situation of the Sinti and Roma has been evidenced by two comprehensive social science studies from 1978 and 1982. No further studies of the kind have been made, but locally restricted investigations reveal that the Sinti and Roma's precarious situation is being perpetuated. The findings show that up to 30 percent of the children are placed in special needs schools, 30 percent of the adults have had no school education, and a further 50 percent had left school, before gaining a leaving certificate. The standard of residential accommodation for a large section of the Sinti and Roma was found to be below the currently accepted minimum level.

In the mid-1980s, a change of policy within the municipalities was initiated, leading to special school and job training measures, as well as local housing programmes, tailored to the Sinti and Roma population. However, the social situation improved only slightly for these people, who had lived in Germany for generations.

A 2007 UNICEF study of the condition of children from Roma families in Germany presented a gloomy picture of prospects for young people, because they "have great difficulty creating a successful life for themselves in conditions where job training provision and the labour market are unfavourable for the young. In many cases, continuing widespread notions about gypsy stereotypes and their background in publicly scorned residential areas also impede the search [for] a job or a training place".

In addition to this, socially and professionally successful Sinti and Roma move away from their old living settlements, which are consequently in danger of becoming "retreat areas for the losers. . . . What occurs here with respect to a minority of the German Sinti is a development that is also known in the whole society: the tendency towards urban segregation according to economic levels".

Sinti and Roma, who have immigrated since the eastern expansion of the EU, continue to live in extremely miserable conditions, despite there being no openly visible slum dwellings and large-scale camps in Germany in contrast to France and Italy.

They have already been subject to murderous attacks in Slovakia and Hungary.

Roma who had fled Bulgaria and Romania gathered in Berlin last year [2009]. They earned themselves a little money by cleaning the windows of cars waiting at the traffic lights on the city's major ring roads. Lacking regular accommodation, they spent the nights outdoors in a park, before being bundled off to an asylum-seekers hostel by the municipal authority. Roma from southeastern Europe have also camped in Berlin parks again this year.

According to a report on the Bavarian radio, as many as 500 Roma have taken up jobs as day workers. As the right of "freedom of movement for employees" has only been implemented in Germany—in contrast to France—since this year, these people are denied work permits, although they are citizens of the European Union. They are therefore forced to work on the "black labour market" on construction sites and in cleaning jobs. Their residence in Germany is thus regarded by the state as illegal, and they face continual harassment from the city authorities.

Considering the Roma in Europe, essayist Karl-Markus Gauss remarked in *Der Zeit* that, "[A]part from the relatively short period of their persecution by the Nazis, their situation has never been so bad in all their history" as it is now. Not only in France have Roma become the target of racist campaigns; they have already been subject to murderous attacks in Slovakia and Hungary. It is significant that the Brussels summit [a summit of EU leaders] resolved, "to try to develop a long-term strategy at the next meeting so that a solution to the problem can be found". Thus, the EU recalls even in its use of language the dark era of Roma persecution, when the "problem" was seen exclusively in terms of ethnicity.

In Australia, Discrimination Against Indigenous People Contributes to Their Ill Health

Yin Paradies

Yin Paradies is a research fellow at the Menzies School of Health Research and Centre for Health and Society at the University of Melbourne in Australia. In the following viewpoint, he argues that indigenous people in Australia are discriminated against on many levels, including employment, education, and housing. Paradies asserts that the indirect effects of these practices on the indigenous peoples are ill health, and even death. More directly, they are not given adequate access to health care or the means to maintain good health.

As you read, consider the following questions:

1. According to the author, how does the average life expectancy of indigenous people compare to that of other Australians?

2. How does the per capita spending on health care for indigenous people compare to that of other Australians, as stated in the viewpoint?

3. What does the author say are some misconceptions of indigenous people?

Yin Paradies, "Discrimination Against Indigenous People," *VicHealth Letter*, no. 7, Winter 2007. www.vichealth.vic.gov.au. Reprinted by permission.

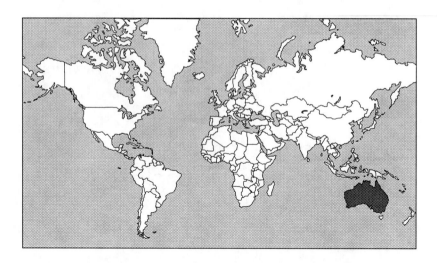

Indigenous people are one of the most disadvantaged groups in Australian society, suffering from high rates of unemployment and incarceration, low income, substandard housing and poor educational outcomes. Together with intergenerational trauma, this material deprivation results in a high burden of ill health and mortality, including a life expectancy that is approximately 17 years less than other Australians.

A History of Discrimination

Such inequality stems from a history of discrimination that includes genocide and alienation as well as loss of land, culture and human rights. Colonisation of Australia occurred over many decades, as waves of white settlers invaded indigenous lands. Australia's pastoral industry was predicated on the theft of indigenous land, the murder of indigenous people who were using scarce resources, and finally exploitation of those who survived as an unpaid labour force (including the sexual abuse of women).

After this early period of Australian history, colonisation continued through government efforts to monitor and control the socialisation, mobility and reproduction of indigenous people through either protection or assimilation. This resulted in no less than 67 definitions of indigenous people in Australian legislation. The following description captures the profound effect that such definitions had:

> *In 1935 a fair-skinned Australian of part-indigenous descent was ejected from a hotel for being an Aboriginal. He returned to his home on the mission station to find himself refused entry because he was not an Aboriginal. He tried to remove his children but was told he could not because they were Aboriginal. He walked to the next town where he was arrested for being an Aboriginal vagrant and placed on the local reserve. During the Second World War he tried to enlist but was told he could not because he was Aboriginal. He went interstate and joined up as a non-Aboriginal. After the war he could not acquire a passport without permission because he was Aboriginal. He received exemption from the Aborigines Protection Act and was told that he could no longer visit his relations on the reserve because he was not an Aboriginal. He was denied permission to enter the Returned Servicemen's Club because he was.*

Systematic Racism

Although such overt forms of control are now defunct, unfortunately there is considerable evidence of continued systemic racism against indigenous people in the policies and practices of Australian governments and institutions.

For example, contrary to the myth of 'buckets of money' poured into indigenous health, the real picture is one of underfunding. Although indigenous people have mortality rates three to five times greater than other Australians, per capita spending on indigenous health is only 1.2 times that of the non-indigenous population. Recent studies have shown that even within existing hospital services indigenous patients are not receiving the same quality of medical care as their non-indigenous counterparts, with systemic racism identified as a possible cause.

Ratio of Indigenous to Non-Indigenous Outcomes, 2001		
	Indigenous	Non-Indigenous
Population aged over 55 years (%)	0.31	1.00
Post-(secondary) school qualification (% adults)	0.30	1.00
Never attended school (% adults)	5.21	1.00
Household size	1.38	1.00
Home owner or purchaser (% population)	0.27	1.00
Median income (household)	0.77	1.00
Median income (individual)	0.62	1.00
Private sector employment (% adults)	0.50	1.00
Full-time employment (% adults)	0.56	1.00
Labour force participation rate (% adults)	0.84	1.00
Employment to population ratio (% adults)	0.66	1.00
Unemployment rate (% labour force)	2.70	1.00

TAKEN FROM: Yin Paradies, "Discrimination Against Indigenous People," *VicHealth Letter*, vol. 7, Winter 2007.

The state of indigenous housing has many parallels. In 1994, it was estimated that more than $3 billion was required to address the backlog of housing and infrastructure needs. In comparison, the 2007–08 federal budget provides approximately an additional $300 million over four years. Meanwhile, indigenous people are discriminated against in the provision of existing housing services.

Misconceptions of indigenous people as being welfare dependent, more likely to drink alcohol and as getting special 'government handouts' still abound, serving to fuel racist attitudes and behaviour. Such continued racism against indigenous people is borne out by survey research. Indigenous people in a 2001 survey reported racism at twice the rate of non-indigenous Australians including experiences of being treated with disrespect and being discriminated against in shops and restaurants.

Indigenous people are discriminated against in the provision of existing housing services.

Recent research has indicated that racism can have a direct association with ill health. A review of existing research in this field found that racism is particularly detrimental to mental health. Research in Australia shows that for indigenous people the stress caused by being the target of racism is associated with chronic conditions such as diabetes, heart disease and cancer, as well as smoking, substance use, psychological distress and poor self-assessed health status.

Such stark evidence underlines the need to know more about the extent and nature of racism in Australia, to better gauge its impact on population health and to discover effective approaches to reducing racial and cultural-based discrimination.

India's Caste System Still Promotes Discrimination of Schoolchildren

D.P. Bhattacharya

D.P. Bhattacharya is a contributing writer for India Today *and* India Express. *In the following viewpoint, Bhattacharya reports on the plight of dalit children in government schools in rural Gujarat. The students complain that the teachers reinforce the caste discrimination by preventing them from drinking from the common vessel and by ordering them to clean the school, particularly the toilets—a task closely related to manual scavenging, a job or "social responsibility" traditionally reserved for dalit families. The minister for social justice and empowerment claims that no one has complained, but the executive director of a dalits rights organization claims that dalits have been complaining and asking the government for help for a long time but to no avail. Students experiencing such treatment at school often drop out, but they continue to receive degrading treatment outside of school.*

As you read, consider the following questions:

1. What is the name of the family that the author mentions as belonging to the dalit class?

2. Who is Manjula Pradeep—what organization does he belong to and what does he do in that organization?

D.P. Bhattacharya, "Govt Teachers Force Dalit Kids to Clean Toilets," *India Today*, August 18, 2009. Courtesy: Mail Today. Reproduced by permission.

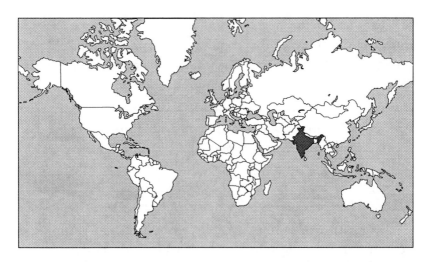

3. How many manual scavengers are there in the state of Gujarat?

They were born Dalits and their schools make sure they never forget that.

Children belonging to the Valmiki caste are forced to clean toilets—a task 'way too beneath the dignity of the upper-caste students'—by their teachers at government schools in rural Gujarat.

The 'educators', who are supposed to dispel prejudices and instill confidence, instead make Dalit children to do the ignominious jobs forcing them to drop out of school sooner or later.

Dalit kids who rallied together in Ahmedabad on Monday against discrimination told of their caste woes, including the practice of untouchability still practiced by many teachers in Gujarat.

Despite the protestations of fair play by minister for social justice and empowerment Fakir Vaghela, a 12-year-old boy from Surendranagar insists he was hit by his teacher because he dared to drink water from the common vessel at school. "I was going to take a sip from the vessel when the teacher hit me with a ruler on my back," says Vishnu Chavda.

"See, he hit me here," Vishnu says, showing his back. His innocent face betrays the anguish that comes from suffering indignations for as long as he could remember and that too for a reason way beyond his comprehension.

The 'educators', who are supposed to dispel prejudices and instill confidence, instead make Dalit children to do the ignominious jobs forcing them to drop out of school sooner or later.

Being born to a Valmiki family, Vishnu's school has wasted no time in exposing him to "the social reality he has to live with". Like almost all other parts in Gujarat, in his Velevada village of Surendranagar district, manual scavengers from his Valmiki community are discriminated against openly.

"Our teachers ask us to clean the school," Vishnu says nonchalantly.

"Others clean classrooms but I am asked to clean the toilet," he says.

Vishnu is not alone. The story is the same across the state, as 15-year-old Gautam Dodiya from Bhavnagar's Umrala block and 13-year-old Gautam Valmiki of Patan district's Harij town reiterate.

But Vaghela claims he has . . . never heard of any such discrimination.

"There is no such thing happening as far as I know," says the minister. His defence is that he never received any such complaint before. "If someone had written to me, I would have commissioned an inquiry." But the 1,000 students who came to voice their plight in Monday's rally at Sabarmati Gandhi Ashram organised by Navsarjan, a pan-Gujarat Dalit rights organisation, disagree.

The minister says he never received complaints about discrimination but activists claim they have been knocking on the government's doors for long.

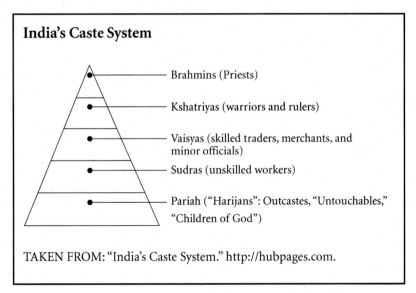

India's Caste System

Brahmins (Priests)

Kshatriyas (warriors and rulers)

Vaisyas (skilled traders, merchants, and minor officials)

Sudras (unskilled workers)

Pariah ("Harijans": Outcastes, "Untouchables," "Children of God")

TAKEN FROM: "India's Caste System." http://hubpages.com.

"We have been taking this issue up with the state government for years now but to no avail. It simply turns a blind eye to the existence of manual scavenging in the state," says Manjula Pradeep, executive director, Navsarjan.

Manjula points out that many students from the community eventually drop out of schools because of such humiliations.

Most of these children are made to drag carcasses of small animals like cats and dogs, every time one dies in the village.

"We have many instances where children refuse to go to school because they can't take such insults any more," she says.

"They are made to sit in the last row in class, made to do the dirtiest of works and called Bhangis and Chamars. Why would anyone want to go to school after that?" she asks.

"We organised this rally to give voice to these kids, whose plight otherwise go unnoticed in the state," she adds.

But it's not only in schools that Dalit children are exposed to the social hierarchy.

They are reminded of their 'position' outside the institutions as well. Being born to Valmiki families comes with the 'social responsibility' of manual scavenging.

Most of these children are made to drag carcasses of small animals like cats and dogs, every time one dies in the village.

With 65,000 manual scavengers, Gujarat is the state with the third-highest number of manual scavengers in the country.

Periodical Bibliography

The following articles have been selected to supplement the diverse views presented in this chapter.

Timothy Chui	"Filipinos Hit Streets as Race Row Rumbles On," *Standard* (Hong Kong), April 6, 2009.
Charlotte Gill	"Black People 'Are 26 Times More Likely to Be Stopped by Police,'" *Mail Online* (UK), October 18, 2010.
Michael J. Jordan	"Why the US Will Boycott Global Racism Conference," *Christian Science Monitor*, April 19, 2009.
Abdalla el-Kurebe	"Albinos Have Suffered Neglect, Says Shagari," *Vanguard* (Lagos), July 19, 2010.
John Langmore	"Opportunity to End Racism Goes to Waste," *Age* (Melbourne, Australia), April 21, 2009.
Chandra Muzaffar	"Marwa Murder Puts Focus on Islamophobia," *New Straits Times* (Malaysia), July 14, 2009.
Peter Mwaura	"Christian Colleges Use Discriminatory Criteria in Admitting New Students," *Daily Nation* (Nairobi), October 22, 2010.
Kathleen Parker	"You'll Love Diversity—Or Else," *Washington Post*, April 19, 2009.
Navi Pillay	"Racism and the World Cup," *New Era* (Namibia), June 10, 2010.
Bob C. Rutarindwa	"Time to Kick Out Discrimination," *New Times* (Rwanda), February 18, 2010.
Harriet Sherwood	"Dozens of Israeli Rabbis Back Call to Forbid Sale of Property to Arabs," *Guardian* (London), December 7, 2010.

GLOBALVIEWPOINTS

CHAPTER 4

Cultural and
Religious Discrimination

Religious Discrimination Remains a Problem Throughout the World

Jonathan Fox

Jonathan Fox is the author of A World Survey of Religion and the State. *In the following viewpoint, Fox says that despite lower overall rates of human rights violations, more people throughout the world face stigma because of their religious beliefs and practices. Although he attributes much of this increase to fear of cultural infiltration, he acknowledges that each country has its own particular reasons for discriminating against religious minorities. Fox asserts that the impact of religion on world cultures has not and will not subside in the near future, as some social scientists have predicted.*

As you read, consider the following questions:

1. By what percentage did the average level of religious discrimination increase between 1990 and 2002?

2. According to the author, which states have the highest levels of religious discrimination?

3. What percentage of Muslim majority states declare Islam their official religion?

Jonathan Fox, "Religious Discrimination: A World Survey," *Journal of International Affairs*, vol. 61, no. 1, Fall/Winter 2007, pp. 47–48, 51–55, 59–62. Reproduced by permission.

Religious discrimination is a phenomenon that has existed for millennia but has recently been receiving increasing attention for two reasons. First, a reexamination of secularization theory in the last two decades of the 20th century and the impact of the September 11 [2001] attacks compelled theorists to turn their attention to the issue of religion in international affairs. More specifically, religion is a topic that had been marginalized by the social sciences for most of the 20th century. In fact, in a body of theory known alternatively as modernization and secularization theory, many social scientists predicted the demise, or at least a weakening, of religion as a significant social and political force. This often included expectations that religion would move from the public sphere to the private sphere. Mainstream social scientists, especially political scientists and sociologists, began to seriously question this set of assumptions only in the last two decades of the 20th century.

September 11, 2001, Was a Catalyst

Mainstream international relations theory went even further. Rather than developing a body of theory that predicted religion's decline, it simply did not address the topic of religion. Some would even argue that the post-Westphalian state system and the discipline of international relations were founded on the belief that the era of religion causing international wars had ended. While this argument may be extreme, it is clear that articles written before September 11 in major international relations journals rarely addressed religion as a significant factor in international relations. Also, when religion was addressed in 20th century international relations theory, it was generally addressed as a subcategory of some other secular phenomenon such as terrorism, culture or civilizations.

Clearly September 11 was not the sole cause of the reevaluation of the role of religion in international relations. Some international relations theorists began to grapple with religion before September 11. It is even likely that had September 11th not occurred, the growing evidence of religion's influence in international relations, combined with the increasing attention given to the issue by other branches of the social sciences, would have eventually resulted in the issue becoming more mainstream. However, September 11 certainly served as a catalyst that spurred a speedy and dramatic surge in research on the role of religion in international relations. This surge was not limited to issues directly related to September 11, such as the threat of radical Islam and the religious causes of terrorism, violence and conflict. Rather, September 11 facilitated a paradigm shift that removed the taboo of openly relating religion to international relations, and opened the floodgates to research on diverse aspects of religion's influence in international relations. This includes issues such as the role of religion on diplomacy, economic development, globalization, voting on foreign policy issues in the U.S. Congress, as well as the religious origins of secularism in Europe. It also spurred attempts to adopt major international relations theories to accommodate religion.

Of the 175 states in the study, fifty-five increased the extent of religious discrimination.

The second reason for the increasing attention given to religious discrimination is the changes in the nature of sovereignty in the past few decades. While at one time a state's domestic policy was considered only an internal matter, aspects of domestic policy are now part of the international agenda. In fact, mistreatment of minorities is becoming a justification for international intervention in a state's affairs. While currently this generally includes only the worst human rights violations, this reflects a concrete change in international norms that makes discrimination against minorities, including religious discrimination, an international issue. . . .

The Extent of Religious Discrimination

In the modern era, with its pressure to abide by human rights standards, one might expect religious discrimination to become increasingly less common. Past social science expectations of religion's decline would lead to a similar conclusion. . . . Yet, . . . the opposite is the case.

Overall, the average level of religious discrimination in the world rose by 11.4 percent between 1990 and 2002. It also increased within each religious tradition and each world region other than Latin America, where it remained the same. Of the 175 states in the study, fifty-five increased the extent of religious discrimination. This includes a diverse set of states including Chad, China, France, Iceland, India, Kuwait, Japan, Romania and Venezuela. However, religious discrimination also decreased in seventeen states. Many of those with the most dramatic decreases, such as Ethiopia (from 18 to 3) and South Africa (from 6 to 0), experienced significant democratization during this period. Overall, these results provide evidence of a large-scale trend of an increase in religious discrimination.

Overall, these results provide evidence of a large-scale trend of an increase in religious discrimination.

The second method analyzes the percentage of states that engage in any religious discrimination. This is important and distinct from average levels of discrimination because the divide between engaging and not engaging in religious discrimination is a crucial one. The results show that 69.7 percent of states engaged in religious discrimination in 1990, as did 74.1 percent in 2002. This represents an increase of nine states. Thus, both methods of analyzing this data show that religious discrimination is both nearly ubiquitous and increasing.

There is certainly some variation across states with different religious majorities as well as across different world regions. Among religious traditions, there is some question over which category engages in the most religious discrimination. On one hand, states with a Muslim religious tradition have the highest average levels of religious discrimination. On the other hand, a larger proportion of Orthodox Christian–majority states engage in religious discrimination, and in 2002 all of them did. The major difference between the two is one of distribution. The top four scoring states in 2002 on the religious discrimination variable—Iran, the Maldives, Saudi Arabia and the Sudan—are Muslim-majority states, as are seven of the top ten. However, there are some Muslim-majority states in Africa, including the Gambia, Senegal and Sierra Leone, that do not engage in any religious discrimination. In contrast, all Orthodox Christian–majority states engage in religious discrimination, but the average levels of religious discrimination are lower in Orthodox Christian–majority states than in Muslim-majority states.

The variation across world regions is less ambiguous. Middle Eastern states evidently have the highest levels of religious discrimination based both on average levels of religious discrimination and the proportion of states that engage in religious discrimination. The region includes the top two scoring states, Saudi Arabia and Iran.

The fact that there has been a significant increase in religious discrimination between 1990 and 2002 is particularly interesting in that such is not the case regarding other types of human rights violations. An examination of changes in observance of twelve types of human rights between 1990 and 2002 based on the Cingranelli-Richards (CIRI) Human Rights Dataset, . . . shows that respect for other types of human rights has increased during this period. Unlike the RAS [Religion and State project] discrimination variable, which measures the extent of discrimination, the CIRI data set gives a higher score to states that observe human rights. Of the twelve types of human rights included in this analysis, ten increased

Freedom Must Apply to All Faiths and None

If we really believe in freedom of thought, conscience and religion, this must include the right to the faith or belief of one's choice, the right to no faith and to be a heretic.

Proportionate limits on this precious liberty don't arise because a minority causes irritation or even offence. We interfere when someone is harming others, or in the workplace when, for instance, their faith or clothing prevents them doing their job.

Shami Chakrabarti,
"Freedom Must Apply to All Faiths and None,"
Times *(London), January 19, 2010.*

between 1990 and 2002, including five types that have statistical significance. The other two types of human rights dropped only slightly Also, the composite variable, which combines all twelve measures, shows a significant increase in overall human rights observances between 1990 and 2002. Thus, the increase in religious discrimination during this period stands out as the exception. . . .

Nearly all other types of human rights violations have decreased while religious discrimination has increased.

Six Main Factors

The results of this study show that religious discrimination— defined as restrictions placed on the practice of religion or religious institutions—has been both prevalent and increasing, at least between 1990 and 2002. This is true regardless of religious tradition, world region and regime type, though there is certainly diversity in the specific patterns of religious discrimination both within and between these religious traditions and regions. This also runs counter to an increase in human rights observance by states on other types of human rights during the same period.

While uncovering all of the reasons and motivations for the presence of an increase in the extent of religious discrimination is not a realistic goal, an analysis of six overlapping and reinforcing factors can help explain religious discrimination in the world. First, that a state may wish to protect its indigenous culture from outside influence is found across world regions and religious traditions. For instance, the indigenous cultures of the Orthodox Christian–majority states of the former Soviet bloc were significantly eroded during the Communist era. Yet, since the end of that era, many of them have followed explicit policies of reestablishing indigenous cultures. This involves supporting the Orthodox Church and other religions with a long historical presence in the state, combined with severely restricting religions considered new to the state.

Second, states such as Georgia and Russia, with Muslim minorities, may fear religious challenges to the state itself. Regardless of whether or not the fear that a minority religion poses a threat to the state is accurate or not, it is certain that this fear exists and that states act on it.

These first two motivations fit well with the finding that nearly all other types of human rights violations have decreased while religious discrimination has increased. These motivations are also consistent with the pattern that most religious discrimination focuses on the public expression of religion and religious institutions rather than the private practice of religion. Public religious expression by nonindigenous minority religions and their religious institutions can both be seen as polluting an indigenous culture and as proof that certain minority religions pose a threat to the state. In contrast, the twelve types of nonreligious human rights violations assessed in this study do not focus on restrictions placed on culture. It is even possible that these types of human rights violations are increasing against certain types of religious minorities, but decreasing overall. The increase of "arrests, detention and harassment" of religious minorities based on the RAS variable combined with a drop in political imprisonment and extrajudicial killings in the CIRI general human rights variables indicate that this may be the case. Thus, the international pressure for improved human rights has been effective, except in cases where states perceive a threat to their rule or their indigenous culture.

Third, many states have policies of monitoring and restricting religions they consider dangerous. This overlaps with the previous explanation but is distinct in that some religions may be considered not only nonindigenous but also particularly dangerous. This pattern often manifests itself in both Western Europe and the former Soviet bloc as an explicit antisect or anticult policy. Twenty-two percent of these states, distributed evenly between the two regions, are coded by the RAS data set as having an explicit antisect policy. This type of policy is less common but present in other world regions. There are certainly sects such as David Koresh's Branch Davidians and Japan's Aum Shinrikyo sects which have proven dangerous. Other popular targets of this type of legislation include Sung Myung Moon's Unification Church and the Church of Scientology which are sometimes perceived as sects that exert unhealthy influences on their followers. However, when countries compile a list of sects and cults, these lists often include religions that are considered mainstream elsewhere such as Seventh-Day Adventists, Mormons, Quakers, Jehovah's Witnesses, Hasidic Jews and Pentecostalism. Thus, this type of legislation is often targeted at nonindigenous religions rather than sects that are perceived to be dangerous.

Fourth, many states may link religion to national identity. This is particularly true of states with Muslim majorities, 57.4 percent of which declare Islam the official religion. Also, 51.1

percent of all Muslim states ban conversion away from Islam. A few, like Saudi Arabia and Kuwait link citizenship to Islam. Interestingly, no Christian states place restrictions on conversion away from Christianity. Of the twenty-nine states which are coded as restricting conversions away from the majority religion, twenty-four are Muslim majority states, three are Buddhist majority states, one, Nepal, is Hindu and the last is China. However, the link between nationalism and religion is present in many states that do not ban conversion away from the majority religion including many Western states. This nationalist preference for a certain religion could potentially motivate restrictions on other religions.

This type of legislation is often targeted at nonindigenous religions rather than sects that are perceived to be dangerous.

Fifth, religious institutions and governments often participate in a classic symbiotic relationship where religious elites and institutions support the state's legitimacy and, in return, the government and political elites support the religious institutions. Some examples of this relationship include the United Kingdom and Greece. This relationship is manifest in a number of forms of government support of religious institutions, including material support, legal privileges and preferred access to public schools. It is also manifest in restrictions placed on other religions.

Sixth, state adherence to religious doctrine can result in religious discrimination. Religious doctrines often call for the superiority of their religion. The potential link between such superiority and religious discrimination is straightforward.

Religion Remains Significant

While these six potential motivations for religious discrimination are not exhaustive, they arguably explain a large proportion of the religious discrimination that exists across the world. There is no doubt that each state has its own unique history and the specific motivations for religious discrimination vary from state to state. However, most of these motivations are likely variations on the six outlined here.

All of this runs counter to the 19th- and 20th-century predictions by social scientists that religion would decline as an important social factor. The general presence and rise of religious discrimination, even as other forms of human rights violations decrease, counter these predictions on an empirical level. Also, each of the six potential motivations for religious discrimination, all of which are certainly present in a significant number of states, show that religion remains deep-seated within politics and culture in general, as well as in the motivations behind government policies in particular.

The statistically significant increase in religious discrimination between 1990 and 2002, while not sufficient to reach definitive conclusions regarding the future of religion in the political arena led, nevertheless, to some tentative and qualified predictions. These increases indicate that religious discrimination and, by implication, the general influence of religion in the political arena [are] likely to last for the foreseeable future. Also, as long as the six motivations for religious discrimination discussed here remain, there is a likelihood that religious discrimination will continue to rise.

European Religious Minorities Need Legal Protection Against Discrimination

Stella Coglievina

The European Network Against Racism (ENAR) is a coalition of more than six hundred nongovernmental organizations (NGOs) working toward ending racism throughout the European Union (EU). In the following viewpoint, ENAR argues that as the population of the EU becomes more diverse, religious discrimination increases. Although the EU has adopted many measures to prevent discrimination based on religious beliefs and practices, ENAR asserts that not enough is being done to protect vulnerable populations.

As you read, consider the following questions:

1. What percentage of people in the European Union consider themselves followers of a religious domination?
2. What is Islamophobia, according to the viewpoint?
3. As explained in the viewpoint, what is racial profiling?

Generally speaking, discrimination means unfair or disadvantageous treatment on the basis of a personal characteristic. Religious discrimination refers to a disadvantageous

Stella Coglievina, "Fact Sheet 34: Religious Discrimination and Legal Protection in the European Union," edited by Tansy Hutchinson and Guidon Van Emden, European Network Against Racism (ENAR), October 2007. http://cms.horus.be/files/99935/MediaArchive/pdf/fs34_religiousdiscrimination_oct2007_en.pdf. Reprinted by permission.

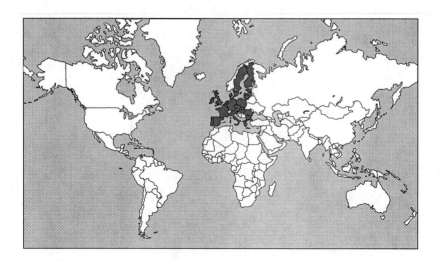

consideration or distinction of people on the basis of their religious affiliation, their personal belief (or non-belief), their faith-based appearance or behaviour or their assumed religious affiliation. Unfair treatment and hostility related to personal beliefs are unfortunately quite common in Europe and they are often engendered by prejudice, especially towards religious minorities. From a legal point of view, defining the concept of religious discrimination is quite complex.

Religion vs. Belief

It is also important to determine what we mean by the terms 'religion' and 'belief'. Generally speaking, religion is defined as "the belief in and worship of a superhuman controlling power, especially a personal God or gods" or as a professed system of faith, including beliefs, observance and worship. The term 'belief' is also commonly used, meaning any system of philosophical beliefs or convictions that guide one's life.

Religious discrimination is experienced through, for example, prejudice, unfair treatment, harassment or forms of violence based on a person's religion or belief. In today's European society we observe hate speech and religiously aggravated crimes, attacks on places of worship and violation of places like cemeteries, as well as anti-Semitic incidents, acts of violence and physical attacks against religious and racial minorities. Some minority groups are also subject to racial and religious profiling and police misconduct towards them.

People are often subject to discrimination, prejudice and violence on the basis of multiple grounds. For example, women belonging to ethnic or religious minorities can be victims of discrimination on the basis both of their gender and their religion or race. The intersection between race and religion is particularly common in today's Europe: on one hand because some groups are characterized both by ethnic/national origin and by religious/cultural backgrounds; on the other hand because frequently it is difficult to distinguish between racist and religious prejudice.

Discrimination on grounds of religion or belief could also refer to differences in the treatment of a person in the enjoyment of her/his fundamental right to freedom of religion or belief.

The intersection between race and religion is particularly common in today's Europe.

Religious Diversity and Discrimination in Europe

Religious discrimination is a problem that is increasingly coming to the fore in today's European societies. With its increasing diversity, Europe is facing a more varied religious landscape than ever before. Migrants, refugees and asylum seekers from different cultural and religious backgrounds have added to previously existing religious diversity, leading to a greater urgency to accommodate diverse religious needs, and to tackle the problem of religious discrimination at all levels of society. Essential to the picture of religious diversity in Europe are the foundation stones of the human rights to religious freedom and to freedom from discrimination on the grounds of religion or belief.

According to the *Eurobarometer Report on Discrimination* [*Special Eurobarometer 263* "Discrimination in the European Union"], a survey issued in January 2007, 44% of Europeans feel that discrimination on grounds of religion or belief is currently widespread in Europe and 64% perceive racial discrimination as a largely common problem. Roma, Sinti and Travellers; third country nationals, particularly undocumented migrants and asylum seekers; the Jewish community and the Muslim community are particularly vulnerable to racial and religious discrimination.

For these communities, religious identity is commonly perceived to be closely connected to racial and ethnic identity: It is often difficult to distinguish between discrimination on the grounds of religion and discrimination on the grounds of racial or ethnic origin. This intersection is particularly strong in the case of, for instance, the Jewish community, which experiences discrimination not only on the grounds of religion but also of ethnic, national or perceived racial characteristics.

With its increasing diversity, Europe is facing a more varied religious landscape than ever before.

Europe's Religious Population

Few reliable statistics exist about the presence of different religious groups in Europe, largely because most European countries do not include questions on religious affiliation in their censuses. According to some recent polls, 73% of the EU [European Union] population consider themselves believers or belong to a religious denomination: Among them, an estimated 66.4% identify as Roman Catholic, 21% Protestant, 6.6% Orthodox Christian, 3% belong to other Christian denominations and 3% belong to other religions (mostly Judaism, Islam and Hinduism). Almost 27% declare themselves to be atheist or agnostic. Other religious communities are also present in Europe, such as Sikhs, Buddhists and other religious groups like Bahá'i, nonconformist denominations and charismatic groups. Some new movements also consider themselves as religious groups. These include forms of Scientism or New Age groups. It should be noted, however, that as we do not have reliable statistics, it is difficult to be exhaustive regarding the range of religious minorities present in the EU.

Some surveys have provided estimates of the number of people belonging to the Islamic faith. This number has increased in many countries; even though there is a lack of data, it appears this increase is due to different factors including migration flows. In some EU Member States, such as Denmark, Italy, Germany, Bulgaria and the Netherlands, Islam is becoming the second or third largest religion in the country. It is often the main religion of some immigrant populations.

Figures on religious observance vary considerably between the different EU countries. In Greece, Malta and Slovenia, for example, a very large majority of the population (between 95% and 98%) considers itself religious, while in Hungary, Latvia, France and the Netherlands the percentage of nonbelievers surpasses 40–45%. Religious affiliation also varies. In some countries (e.g., France, Austria, Italy, Spain and Portugal) the main religious community is Roman Catholic, while in Romania, Bulgaria and Greece the largest affiliation is with various Orthodox churches. Meanwhile, Germany, the United Kingdom, Denmark and Sweden are historically more Protestant countries. The presence of Islam also varies in the Member States: from a very small presence (0.05% of the total population in Portugal, and 0.1% in Poland, the Czech Republic and Hungary) to an estimated 4% in Germany, 5.7% in the Netherlands, and up to 10–11% in France and Bulgaria.

Religious Discrimination in Europe

The presence of such religious diversity in today's Europe has led to increasing contact between religious groups, which has sometimes revealed deep-seated prejudice and stereotyping leading to tension and even conflict. Religion is, indeed, an essential element in the identity of some of the groups that make up our societies, but it has also been associated with stereotypes or negative pre-conceptions, including the assumption of a so-called 'clash of civilizations'.

Popular discourse and political events, frequently reflected in the media, have negatively linked Islam and terrorism. This has influenced social attitudes and led to a resurgence of racial and religious discrimination. A recent report of the European Monitoring Centre on Racism and Xenophobia (EUMC) found that Muslims are often victims of discrimination, negative stereotyping and of manifestations of prejudice and hatred. These take the form of verbal threats and physical attacks on people and property and racial profiling.

People belonging to religious minorities, especially migrants, also have disproportionately lower incomes and higher rates of unemployment.

The 'war on terror' in particular has created a new source of fear concerning minority communities, especially Muslim ones. Events since September 11 [2001 terrorist attacks on the United States], including the Madrid and London bombings, have heightened these fears and have led to a greater marginalisation and discrimination and to a rise in anti-Muslim sentiment and actions. This phenomenon is commonly termed "Islamophobia". The evidence indicates that there is certainly some impact of the 'war on terror' on the rights to freedom of expression and religion.

People belonging to religious minorities, especially migrants, also have disproportionately lower incomes and higher rates of unemployment. They face difficulties accessing housing and often live in poor neighbourhoods. They suffer from prejudice and experience exclusion or marginalisation in social, political and economic activity and from unfair treatment in public or social services.

There is an increase in hate speech. People manifest pejorative views about certain religious groups, not only in private ideas and speech, but also in public settings and sometimes in political discourse. This represents a vilification of religious feelings and of certain groups, which as a result do not feel free to manifest and practice their religion. Hate speech can also incite acts of violence; in these cases criminal law provides for specific sanctions, but generally these can be applied only in the most extreme cases, where there is a risk of physical violence or public disorder.

There is an increasing level of violence against religious minorities, especially attacks on places of worship, vandalism in cemeteries, hostility and harassment in public debates and popular discourse. There are also assaults on individuals, particularly those belonging to "visible" minorities, who are distinguished by distinctive clothing or other signs of faith and religious identity.

Restrictions on Religious Freedom

Religious freedom is universally recognised and enshrined in many legal instruments; in practice however, there can be a disparity between the guaranteeing of this right and of its enforcement in practice, and therefore a gap remains between the legal commitments and the realities experienced by religious communities. Member States' laws, policy and practice are sometimes part of this problem, such as in the following cases:

'Racial Profiling' is any police or private security practice in which a person is treated as a suspect because of his or her

---

Examples of Religious Discrimination

a) An employer decides not to employ a job applicant because, although he has the skills required for the job, during an interview it becomes apparent that he is a Muslim. This is discrimination on grounds of religion or belief.

b) Students in a school are ridiculed or even physically attacked by reason of their faith. This constitutes religious harassment.

c) A state allows only certain religious organizations to register and to have places of worship: this could lead to discrimination in the individual right to practice a religion or belief.

d) An organization that represents religious minorities organizes a meeting, to which all members are invited, on a Jewish holiday. If there are Jewish participants who are prevented from coming solely by the date of the meeting, then this is a failure to accommodate their religious needs.

European Network Against Racism,
"Religious Discrimination and Legal
Protection in the European Union,"
Fact Sheet No. 34, October 2007. www.flw.ugent.be.

---

race, ethnicity, nationality or religion. The 'war on terror' is again linked to these practices; sometimes it is argued that the aim of national security justifies them, such as when certain people, especially those coming from the Middle East, are required to pass additional security checks because of their ethnicity and religion. In these cases, the external and religious characteristics of targeted people are often blurred and indissociable. Other practices of concern include police checks of mosques and in local Muslim communities, practices which can lead to a restriction of the right to religious freedom.

The issue of registration of religious communities is of particular concern, above all for the 'new religious movements' (sometimes also called 'sects') that often have difficulties in obtaining legal status. While a number of churches and religious communities have a long-standing presence in Europe and have gained a particular status and certain privileges, many others do not receive the same treatment. This can lead to restrictions of the individual right of religious freedom. For example: If some rights (e.g., permission for building a place of worship) are guaranteed by a state only to religious communities that have been recognised, people belonging to non-registered religions can be discriminated against in the exercise of their right to practice their religion.

The issue of religious symbols has also been debated with respect to public schools.

Accommodation of religious diversity and in particular the individual's right to manifest and practice religion is a challenge facing many in Europe today. The increasing religious diversity in Europe has amplified this problem, above all when those needs concern practices that differ from the most common European religious practices and traditions. For example, a common tradition in Europe is to have Sunday as a day of rest. As a consequence, problems arise from the desire to attend religious services at other times during the week. Other issues can come up concerning particular diets or other practices, for example wearing religious symbols or clothes, or the observance of religious holidays.

The issue of religious symbols has also been debated with respect to public schools. In some countries a ban has been imposed on "signs or clothes by which a student ostensibly manifests his or her religious beliefs" (e.g., in France), protecting, in the view of the government, the neutrality and secular character of the public sphere.

European countries have different models of religious education in public schools. Some EU Member States (for instance Austria, Belgium, Germany, Italy, Spain and the UK) provide religious instruction in public schools, organised by the dominant religion in the country. In some countries there are several alternative kinds of religious education, organised by respective recognised religious communities. While religious classes are generally not mandatory, discriminatory attitudes towards minority religions in schools are still a current phenomenon. . . .

Legal Response to Religious Discrimination

The European Community has long been active in the fight against discrimination. Indeed, at the time of its creation one of its most pressing missions was to reconcile a continent divided by nationalist and ethnic conflicts. For many years, European Community law provided protection only against discrimination on the grounds of sex and nationality. Since the 1980s, the issues of racism and racial and religious discrimination have become more prominent in discussions at the European level. As the EU was founded on the principles of liberty, democracy, the rule of law and respect for human rights and fundamental freedoms, the protection of all persons against discrimination is essential to the creation of an area of justice, freedom and security throughout the Union's Member States.

The urgency of combating racism and related intolerance calls for appropriate actions at the European level. Combating racism, xenophobia and religious discrimination can be done more effectively through co-operation between European countries, aiming in concert to eradicate these phenomena from Europe. To achieve this, a number of measures and initiatives were put into practice within the EU, especially during the 1990s. While the EU's anti-discrimination policy during these years was mainly focused on race and ethnicity, in many documents religious discrimination is discussed and mentioned together with racial and ethnic discrimination.

All this notwithstanding, the distinction between racial and religious discrimination has been emphasised by, for instance, the exclusion of the latter from the Racial Equality Directive, as we shall see below, thus playing down the fact that the boundary between these two grounds is not easily drawn. This may be a reflection of the fact that religious matters have generally been considered as a competency of the individual Member States, and were therefore not handled by the European institutions. However, the European Commission in July 2007 launched a consultation to consider a possible new initiative to prevent and combat discrimination outside employment, including on grounds of religion or belief. . . .

The urgency of combating racism and related intolerance calls for appropriate actions at the European level.

A Need for More Intervention

The increasing visibility of religious diversity in Europe has been accompanied by a rise in discrimination and prejudice against ethnic and religious minorities. While a great deal of progress has been made, discrimination on grounds of racial or ethnic origin and religion is still a problem for many people in our societies, although this is difficult to measure accurately due to a lack of data on the religious composition of the population of the EU, particularly as regards minority religions. The European Union has created a framework of legal instruments, policies and initiatives for combating religious and racial discrimination and for promoting equality. Nevertheless, it could be argued that the principles of equality and non-discrimination and the respect for the right to freedom of thought, conscience and religion have not been fully implemented in all Member States.

The paper outlines the complexity of the current legal protection and the remaining gaps in anti-discrimination legislation, highlighting the fact that, as many have argued, the European Union should adopt more comprehensive and more extensive legislation on religious discrimination. It is also recognised that legal instruments alone are not sufficient to grant a broad implementation of the principle of equality or to ensure that commitment to this principle is shared by all people in our society. The role that NGOs [nongovernmental organisations] and associations can play cannot be overstated, both in terms of support for victims of discrimination and in combating prejudice within EU society.

In the European Union, Religious Discrimination in the Workplace Remains a Major Problem

Mahmut Yavaşi

Mahmut Yavaşi is a legal scholar who focuses on religion and international human rights. In the following viewpoint, Yavaşi argues that while the European Union (EU) has passed laws to prevent religious discrimination in the workplace, more needs to be done. The most difficult aspect of eliminating religious discrimination is overcoming the challenges of proving that it exists. Furthermore, Yavaşi asserts, not all religious minorities can easily have their needs met. Unfortunately, religious discrimination in the EU will likely continue unless laws are better enforced.

As you read, consider the following questions:

1. What is *inter alia*?

2. According to the Framework Directive, what does the "principle of equal treatment" mean?

3. What are some specific examples of unfair treatment in employment, according to Weller's study?

Mahmut Yavaşi, "Elimination of Religious Discrimination at Workplace in the EU with Particular Reference to the UK," *Review of International Law and Politics*, vol. 3, no. 10, 2007, pp. 115–116, 121, 123–129. Reprinted by permission.

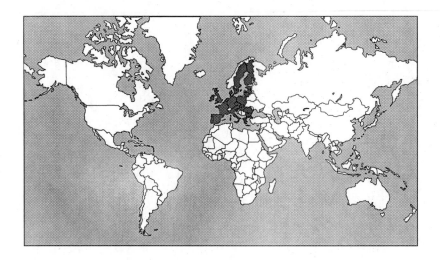

Almost all major human rights treaties forbid discrimination on grounds of religion and a number of EC [European Commission, the executive body of the European Union] Treaty provisions affirm that every form of discrimination must be combated in order to ensure equal treatment at workplace.

The present paper analyses legal background of religious discrimination at workplace in the EU [European Union] and its potential influence on non-Christian employees in the EU.

Treaty Provisions

The concept of fundamental rights was not contained in the original EEC [European Economic Community] Treaty. For the first time, the Single European Act [SEA] made reference to respect for human rights. The Preamble of the SEA subscribes to universal and regional instruments and assuming responsibility for promoting the principles of democracy, the rule of law and respect for human rights. The Preamble of the SEA also states that the EU and the Member States should work together to promote democracy on the basis of the fundamental rights recognized in the constitutions and laws of the Member States, in the Convention for the Protection of

Human Rights and Fundamental Freedoms and the European Social Charter of 18 November 1961, notably freedom, equality and social justice.

The Preamble of the SEA underpins the EU in accordance with the Solemn Declaration [on European Union] of Stuttgart of 19 June 1983. Ten years after than the Declaration, a major step in integrating human rights into the EU's policies was taken with the entry into force of the Treaty on European Union (TEU). Article 2 of the TEU provides that one of the EU's objectives is to strengthen the protection of the rights and interests of the nationals of its Member States through the introduction of a citizenship of the Union. Article 6(1) of the TEU provides that the Union is founded on the principles of liberty, democracy, respect for human rights and fundamental freedoms, and the rule of law, principles which are common to the Member States, and Article 6(2) states that the Union shall respect fundamental rights, as guaranteed by the European Convention for the Protection of Human Rights [and Fundamental Freedoms] and as they result from the constitutional traditions common to the Member States, as general principles of Community law. The TEU stipulates that candidate countries will have to respect these principles to join the Union. This confirms the long-standing practice of the European Court of Justice (ECJ) in using the ECHR [European Court of Human Rights] as an embodiment of the general principles, common to the Member States. In other words, the case law of the ECJ is now reflected in Article 6(2) of the TEU.

Prior to the Treaty of Amsterdam there was no immediate power for the Community to deal with racial or religious discrimination.

The Treaty of Amsterdam marks another significant step forward in integrating human rights into the EU legal order.

The Treaty of Amsterdam reaffirms, in Article 6, that the EU is founded on the principles of liberty, democracy, respect for human rights and fundamental freedoms, and the rule of law, principles which are common to the Member States.

Prior to the Treaty of Amsterdam there was no immediate power for the Community to deal with racial or religious discrimination. Article 13 of the EC Treaty, as introduced by the Treaty of Amsterdam, puts an end to the long debate about Community competence on anti-discrimination matters. It provides a legal basis for the Council, acting unanimously, on a proposal from the Commission and after consultation with the European Parliament, to take "appropriate action" to combat discrimination based on sex, racial or ethnic origin, religion or belief, disability, age or sexual orientation.

The Commission, together with the Council and Parliament, participated in the solemn proclamation of the Charter of Fundamental Rights on 7 December 2000. Article 10 of the EU Charter follows Article 9 of the ECHR on freedom of thought, conscience and religion, and Article 13 has a free-standing provision, along the lines of Protocol No. 12 to the ECHR, which prohibits discrimination on grounds, *inter alia* [among other things] of "religion or belief". The Charter of Fundamental Rights has not been integrated into EU law, and therefore it does not have a clearly identified legal status. However, it may be seen by the ECJ as a source of inspiration which the Community institutions and the Member States when implementing Community obligations must respect. The future of the Charter of Fundamental Rights will inevitably depend on its legal status. However, it should be noted that the Charter contains similar provisions with Protocol 12.

A Framework Directive has been issued under the power, given to Council by Article 13 of the Amsterdam, to outlaw discrimination in employment. Article 1 of the Framework Directive covers, *inter alia*, discrimination on grounds of religion or belief, in relation to employment and occupation only.

The Council has also adopted a Community action programme to combat discrimination in the period from 2001 to 2006. The issues arising from the Framework Directive are among the subjects of this paper. Before going a step further in dealing with the case law of the ECJ, international measures on discrimination that the ECJ has been referring should briefly be dealt with. . . .

The Framework Directive

The EU Framework Directive covers, *inter alia*, discrimination at workplace on grounds of religion or belief. Thus, the Community has, for the first time, stated that the elimination of religious discrimination constitutes a fundamental principle of Community law, as it has said of sex discrimination. The overall effect of above mentioned EC and the EU Charter requires the Framework Directive to be implemented so as to be compatible with the rights set out in the ECHR, Convention No. 111 of the ILO [International Labour Organization], International Covenant on Civil and Political Rights. . . .

The 'principle of equal treatment' shall mean that there shall be no direct or indirect discrimination whatsoever, *inter alia*, on religion or belief, as regards employment and occupation. The protection applies to all employees in relation to conditions of employment conditions for access to employment, to self-employment or to occupation, including selection criteria and recruitment conditions, whatever the branch of activity and at all levels of the professional hierarchy, including promotion; access to all types and to all levels of vocational guidance, vocational training, advanced vocational training and retraining, including practical work experience; employment and working conditions, including dismissals and pay; membership of, and involvement in, an organization of workers or employers, or any organization whose members carry on a particular profession, including the benefits provided by such organizations (Article 3(1) of the Framework Directive).

The concept of discrimination is based on a comparative model of comparing one person who has been less favorably treated than another in a comparable situation on the prohibited grounds or imposing a practice on one person having a particular religion or belief thereby putting them at a particular disadvantage as compared with other persons (Article 2(2)(an) and (b) of the Framework Directive).

Direct Discrimination. Direct discrimination means that employees or job applicants must not be treated less favorably than others because they follow, are perceived to follow, or do not follow a particular (or any) religion or belief. This tends to be obvious discrimination, for example, a Muslim candidate with the best qualifications and experience does not get an interview, but a Christian candidate with [fewer] qualifications does. Treating members of the compared groups equally badly can satisfy the principle. Direct discrimination may only be justified in the very limited circumstances where a genuine occupational requirement can be shown to apply.

In contrast to direct discrimination, indirect discrimination will not be unlawful if it can be justified.

Indirect Discrimination. The concept of indirect discrimination has been developed by case law of the ECJ in respect of sex and nationality.

Indirect discrimination occurs where the effect of certain requirements, conditions or practices imposed by an employer has an adverse impact disproportionally on one group or other. According to Weller P. *et al.* specific examples of unfair treatment in employment that were given by respondents included the following, in England and Wales: Dress restrictions (Muslims, Sikhs, inter-faith); Working on religious days/holidays (Christians, Jains, Jews, NRMs [new religious movements], Pagans, Sikhs); Lack of respect and ignorance of religious customs (Hindus, Jews, Muslims, Zoroastrians); Application and recruitment practices (Christians, Muslims, NRMs, Sikhs, Zoroastrians, inter-faith); Promotion prospects (Sikhs).

In contrast to direct discrimination, indirect discrimination will not be unlawful if it can be justified. To justify it, an employer must show that there is a legitimate aim, (*i.e.*, a real business need) and that the practice is proportionate to that aim (*i.e.*, necessary and there is no alternative means available).

Harassment. Harassment shall be deemed to be a form of discrimination. Harassment occurs when unwanted conduct related to, *inter alia*, religion takes place with the purpose or effect of violating the dignity of a person and of creating an intimidating, hostile, degrading, humiliating or offensive environment. In this context, the concept of harassment may be defined in accordance with the national laws and practice of the Member States (Article 2(3) of the Framework Directive).

As with other grounds of discrimination, the employer is deemed liable for the acts of his employees done in the course of employment, whether or not the employer knew or approved of them. Harassment includes behavior that is offensive, frightening or in any way distressing. It may involve nicknames, teasing, name-calling or other behavior that may not be intended to be malicious but nevertheless is upsetting.

Victimization. Article 11 of the Framework Directive provides that Member States shall introduce into their national legal systems such measures as are necessary to protect employees against dismissal or other adverse treatment by the employer as a reaction to a complaint within the undertaking or to any legal proceedings aimed at enforcing compliance with the principle of equal treatment. In practice, victimization may take place when an individual is treated detrimentally because he or she has made a complaint or intends to make a complaint about discrimination or harassment or has given

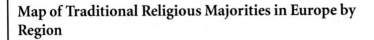

Map of Traditional Religious Majorities in Europe by Region

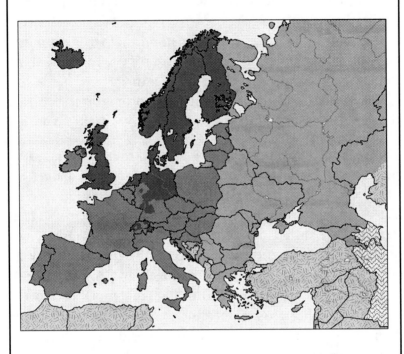

■ Protestant Christianity
■ Catholic Christianity
■ Orthodox Christianity
▨ Sunni Islam
▧ Shia Islam

TAKEN FROM: "Map of Traditional Religious Majorities by Region in Europe," Eupedia, 2004–2009. www.eupedia.com/europe.

evidence or intends to give evidence relating to a complaint about discrimination or harassment.

Putting a complaint petition to the relevant authorities or suing an employer may not only result in administrative punishment but also be considered a reason not to promote the employee. Furthermore, prosecution and investigation of a complaint depends upon the decision of the highest authority of a relevant public institution. If the relevant administrative authority decides that there is no need for investigation, an infringement of any right of public employee cannot be taken before the criminal court. This requirement has to be eliminated to combat discrimination. . . .

The Right to Discrimination on the Grounds of Religion

An employer may lawfully discriminate in selecting employees for a job where being a member of a particular religion or belief is a genuine occupational qualification for the job. The Framework Directive provides that a difference of treatment by an employer that is based on a characteristic related to religion will not constitute discrimination. In very limited circumstances, it will be lawful for an employer to treat people differently if it is a genuine occupational requirement that the job holder must be of a particular religion or belief. If the characteristic in question constitutes a genuine occupational requirement, provided that the objective is legitimate and the requirement is proportional. When deciding if this applies it is necessary to consider the nature of the work and the context in which it is carried out.

It will be lawful for an employer to treat people differently if it is a genuine occupational requirement.

Some employers have an ethos based on a religion or belief. Where employers can show that they are founded on such an ethos they may be able to apply a genuine occupational requirement to jobs where in other circumstances such a requirement would not apply. In these cases the need for a particular religion or belief may not be a 'decisive' factor for the job but employers must still be able to show that it is a requirement of the job in order to adhere to the ethos of the organization and that it is proportionate to apply the requirement. . . .

People spend more time at work than they spend in many other social situations. In order to develop greater productivity and competitiveness, any form of discrimination on the basis of religion, *inter alia*, should be eliminated. With a multireligious EU, there comes a positive responsibility to ensure that economic inclusiveness should be extended to different faith groups. For some thinkers and politicians, Christianity should be a basis of European identity but it should also bear in mind that if we take this as a basis, this will also be a dangerous move that ignores the millions of Europeans who are not religious and, of course, also those who are not Christian.

Human rights are only adequately protected where the nuances of each individual's makeup are recognized and accommodated. Looking at the workplace it is obvious that commonplace rules come into conflict with religious expectations in many different ways. Observant Muslims have to take part in the congregational prayer on Friday and they have to accomplish ritual prayer on normal workdays during the week. Sabbath observant Jews may not wish to work after sunset on Fridays and on Saturdays. Christians may not wish to work on Sundays. Sikhs may be unwilling to observe rules about being clean-shaven.

Limitations of the Framework Directive

The Framework Directive attempts to accommodate some [of] the particularity of all individuals. However, it is unlikely that specific rules that would be equally applicable to all religious groups could be drafted. For example, it may prove impossible for a jurisdiction to recognize all holy days and religious festivals. Therefore, the Framework Directive does not say that employers must provide time and facilities for religious or belief observance, changing break times in order to accommodate fasting, or in laying down rules on dress, uniform, *etc.*, in the workplace. However, employers are required to consider whether their codes, policies, rules and procedures indirectly discriminate against staff of particular religions or beliefs and if so whether reasonable changes might be made. Otherwise, employers could be found guilty of discrimination if they refuse individual requests simply because of the employee's religion or belief.

The Framework Directive does not take into account specific needs of minority religious employees. The problems of Muslim female employees wearing headscarves *inter alia*, should be eliminated and their compatibility with the Framework Directive should be reviewed.

It is extremely difficult for a victim to prove that she or he has suffered discrimination.

Lack of an effective enforcement mechanism for international legal instruments on discrimination is a major problem. It is hoped that the EU's recent Framework Directive will eliminate violation of universally accepted norms, at least, in the EU.

Although legal basis for non-discrimination has partly been established, it is extremely difficult for a victim to prove that she or he has suffered discrimination. Access to justice, insufficient protection against victimization, a poor understanding of equality concepts amongst the judiciary, inadequate and inappropriate remedies are the main topics of the problematic areas.

It seems, now, that non-discrimination right on the basis of religion and belief will automatically be protected as a general principle of Community law. Binding Framework Directive should be enforced more swiftly by national courts, and ultimately by the ECJ. It is to be hoped that the framework directive will succeed in the promotion of religious freedom and the prohibition of religious discrimination and intolerance at workplace.

Yemeni Culture Is Still Dominated by Discrimination

Ola Al-Shami and Marwa Al-Zubairi

Ola Al-Shami and Marwa Al-Zubairi are regular contributors to the Yemen Times *from which the following viewpoint is taken. They argue that as more social classes have been added to Yemeni culture, discrimination has increased. Currently, the class that takes the most abuse is known as the al-muhamasheen (pejoratively as the akhdam). Al-Shami and Al-Zubairi assert that this group is isolated socially and economically. The Yemeni government has done little to remedy the situation and few citizens of other social classes are interested in supporting the rights of the al-muhamasheen.*

As you read, consider the following questions:

1. What does "al-muhamasheen" mean?
2. What are the four main tribes in Yemen?
3. What types of jobs do al-muhamasheen generally do?

Saeeda was a young Yemeni woman from the akhdam. She was working as a street cleaner in Sana'a when a group of men began to harass her. The men ended up slicing Saeeda's neck, killing her, and stabbing her brother in the chest several times. Nothing was done by authorities to investigate or avenge Saeeda's death.

Ola Al-Shami and Marwa Al-Zubairi, "Social Discrimination Still Dominates Yemeni Culture," *Yemen Times*, June 29, 2009. Reprinted by permission.

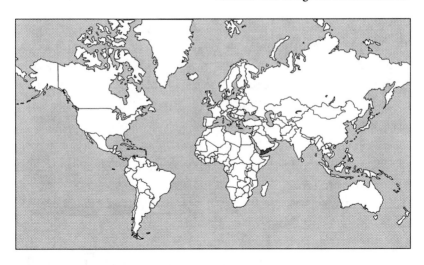

The Emergence of Social Classes

More than 50 decades ago, there were only two visible classes, the Imam and his family who were descendants of the Prophet, and the rest of the public. But after the Imamate rule ended, three classes emerged: the Hashemite or saada, the tribes, known as a'raab or qabael, and the mazaayina, also known as atraaf.

An additional class has emerged, popularly known as the akhdam. This term, however, carries with it a negative stigma, and they prefer to call themselves, al-muhamasheen, or the marginalized ones.

The muhamasheen is the impoverished class. They are isolated socially and economically. They frequently live in places like slums on the outskirts of Sana'a, where there are makeshift homes and no electricity. Children often have limited, if any, access to education, adequate nutrition or sanitation.

The muhamasheen are also often victims of discrimination or prejudice. Children drop out of school because they are looked down upon by their peers. Homes flood when it rains. Ali Izzil Muhammad Obaid told the *New York Times*: "We are surviving but we are not living."

The government has not done much to fix this problem. The Yemeni constitution says, "The state shall guarantee equal opportunities for all citizens in the fields of political, economic, social and cultural activities." It also says Yemeni Society is based in social solidarity, which is based on justice, freedom and equality according to the law.

The muhamasheen are also often victims of discrimination or prejudice.

Although the Yemeni constitution promises equality for all, it doesn't provide it. In articles 24 and 25 of chapter 3 on social and cultural foundations, it says that it will provide the same opportunities to all Yemenis culturally, economically, politically and even socially, but none of this has happened.

The constitution was laid down in 1994 and 15 years later, the situation is as bad as ever.

Prisoners of War

According to Iranian historian Mohammed Hussein Fadhlallah, Ethiopians also known as the Ahbash in Arabic ruled Yemen for 72 years over 1,500 years ago.

During their rule, one of their kings called Abraha wanted to save the Yemeni deteriorating economy then by directing trade and attention to Sana'a instead of Hijaz in what is known today as Saudi Arabia.

He realized that he needed to destroy the Ka'aba and attract world pilgrimage and hence trade towards Yemen by building a magnificent church he called "Al-Qilees."

However, his attack on Mecca failed and he returned to Yemen in 571 A.C. ["after Christ"] while his people in Yemen were fought by a Yemeni leader with support from Persia called Saif bin Thee Yazan.

The Ahbash were then enslaved and made to work in demeaning jobs such as cleaning bathrooms, washing dishes and sweeping streets. They were not allowed to slaughter animals or cook food until recently because they were considered by Yemenis as 'unclean' because of their slavery status.

The mazaayina, however, were. According to renowned 9th-century historian Ibn Al-Saeb Al-Kalbi, the latter were prisoners of war caught during the Islamic expansion towards northern Arabia. This is why they usually have fair skin and blue and green eyes.

They appeared in Yemen many years after the Ahbash slaves and so they were given a slightly higher status through being able to serve in the houses in cooking and slaughtering, or barbers or working in the Turkish baths known as hamams.

The mazaayina are traditionally considered working-class, and work as barbers, entertainers and butchers. However, many work as circumcisers, give injections or administer first aid. They are referred to as doctors by almost all the social classes, especially in the rural areas. The mazaayina also traditionally sing at weddings, help to prepare brides for their wedding day, and serve in wealthy homes.

At the top of the social ladder, the saada claim Hashemite ancestry, dating back to the Prophet Mohammed (P.B.U.H. ["peace be upon him"]). They traditionally work as judges or religious leaders because of their history of access to education and leadership.

The saada and the tribes once kept their distance, but now share a closer relationship. It used to be unacceptable for a saada to marry someone from any tribe. More recently, however, the saada marriage range has expanded, and they are allowed to marry members of the tribes.

Most saada families, however, will not permit their relatives to marry members of the mazaayina or muhamasheen. Neither are members of the tribal class.

Yemeni tribes are divided into four main groups that describe themselves as the descendents of four sheiks: Hashid, Bakil, Hamdan and Madhaj. The tribes are now lead by sheikhs who enforce a tribal system of law. Yemeni sheikhs have their own prisons, arms and soldiers.

Pervasive Discrimination

The last two classes suffer from social discrimination although for the muhamasheen it is much worse because of their dark skin color.

This is a prevalent concept, although they are not necessarily black especially since, over the years, some abandoned children were conceived outside wedlock by qabael or saada and dumped in the akhdam's neighborhood. The akhdam took care of the children as their own and married them with their own, and so with time some families have lighter skin colors because of this.

There are some Yemenis who are of dark skin and those are generally from coastal areas or the valley in Hadhramout. Where they live, they are integrated normally into society but when they travel to other areas in Yemen they are sometimes looked down upon just because they are black, despite the fact that they could be from a higher social class.

However, muhamasheen remain the most discriminated against and are also regularly denied basic rights like property, credit or employment.

Muhamasheen remain the most discriminated against and are also regularly denied basic rights like property, credit or employment.

According to people from rural Taiz, each area or district had its akhdam. Each area's inhabitants were responsible for protecting them, giving them food and shelter in return for the akhdam's services, in the form of domestic work and especially during weddings and social occasions.

The trend was that the akhdam of one area or village were not allowed to work in another. They belonged to a specific territory and had to operate within that.

During weddings for example, their job was to play the drums, sing and entertain the people. They also helped in domestic chores mainly cleaning and serving people.

During the dancing, friends and family would throw money into the lap of the akhdam entertainment leader after gesturing circles with the money on top of the bride or the groom's head. This show was a cultural tradition supposed to break the evil eye, and say, "Your value is above all money."

When the bride or groom dances, family and friends compete to see who can throw in the [most] money. It is a special treat for the akhdam that day.

Outside the wedding seasons, the akhdam earn money by doing services in the village. When there is no work, they can easily go to houses and demand money or food or clothes. Locals were obliged to give them because they were the responsibility of the village.

In recent years, some akhdam went to schools and broke free from this form of unwritten slavery, and some even traveled and worked abroad. But for the majority, especially in the cities, they are still heavily discriminated against and looked down upon.

"These groups face tyrannical treatment from society because of their unknown origins, according to which they are now not allowed to take leading positions in the state, and in the past were not allowed to in the tribe," said Mohammed Al-Khayat, a professor of social studies at the University of Sana'a. "So, they worked in jobs considered as low professions socially."

Challenging the Norm

Challenging social norms is not easy, and in some cases the costs are heavy.

"A man from the saada class wanted to marry his daughter to her relative who was of the a'raab," said Um Ali, an a'raab who asked not to be identified by her full name. "When they

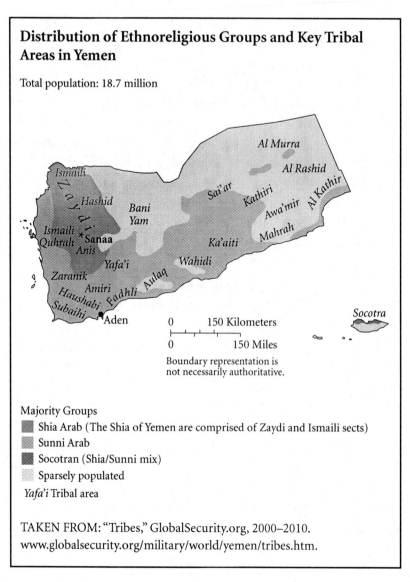

Distribution of Ethnoreligious Groups and Key Tribal Areas in Yemen

Total population: 18.7 million

Al Murra

Al Rashid

Ismaili

Hashid

Bani
Yam

Saï ar

Kathiri

Awa'mir

Al Kathir

Ismaili
Quhrah

Sanaa

Anis

Ka'aiti

Mahrah

Zaranik

Yafa'i

Wahidi

Aulaq

Amiri

Haushabi

Fadhli

Subaihi

Aden

Socotra

0   150 Kilometers

0   150 Miles

Boundary representation is
not necessarily authoritative.

Majority Groups

■ Shia Arab (The Shia of Yemen are comprised of Zaydi and Ismaili sects)
■ Sunni Arab
■ Socotran (Shia/Sunni mix)
□ Sparsely populated
Yafa'i Tribal area

TAKEN FROM: "Tribes," GlobalSecurity.org, 2000–2010.
www.globalsecurity.org/military/world/yemen/tribes.htm.

came to Sana'a to buy the clothes for the bride, her elder brothers who live in Sana'a refused to let the marriage to happen."

"[The brothers] disobeyed their father, who told them of his agreement with his [potential] new son-in-law. They kept on refusing the marriage, which caused the father to be paralyzed for nearly three years which ended in his death."

Some saada think they are too good to socialize with other classes. A saada woman would never invite a neighbor from the tribes over to her house for lunch, and she would never let her children hang out with muhamasheen.

"The saada and qabael interact socially and invite each other to their weddings or celebrations, but it is unheard of to invite mazaayina or akhdam as guests," said Mohammed Noman Al-Hakimi a writer from Taiz. "There is a red line between those two groups and the saada and mazaayina that cannot be crossed."

"In fact if you were to insult someone you would call him 'ya muzayyin,'" he continued. "Even if we were to invite the akhdam, they are generally dirty and don't dress up nicely. As for the mazaayina, it is impossible to even consider inviting them."

Challenging social norms is not easy, and in some cases the costs are heavy.

A wealthy mazaayina man wanted to marry a saada woman and since her family would never accept him, he changed his last name to one of the common names of saada families. He claimed he had no family members or relatives. The ruse worked because he lived in a town where nobody knew his past. Her family agreed and the couple married.

After three years, the man and his wife traveled to Egypt to visit her brother. He met another man whose last name was the same as the mazaayina man's acclaimed surname.

The other man doubted his origin and asked him about specific details known only to those from the family. The mazaayina was forced to confess that he lied in order to marry. His wife's family then forced him to divorce her, although they had just had a baby together a few months before.

Society's Apathy and Winds of Change

Kevin Aldrich, a teacher at the Sana'a International School, said that he tried to organize a charity walk to benefit the muhamasheen. He cancelled the event because people lacked interest or enthusiasm. The students were simply not interested in this topic, he said.

Increasingly humanitarian and rights-based organizations in Yemen are executing projects to improve their situation.

But when another teacher, David Stanton, organized a charity walk to raise money for the Arabian leopards which are in danger of extinction, people jumped at the opportunity and raised USD [United States dollars] 5,000 that day.

There are some NGOs [nongovernmental organizations] made by the marginalized communities mostly from akhdams who have organized themselves in order to change their conditions such as Amer and Uqbi Association. Increasingly humanitarian and rights-based organizations in Yemen are executing projects to improve their situation. A documentary has been released recently by WITNESS and Sisters' Arabic Forum for Human Rights on the plight of akhdam and injustice happening to that community in Yemen. The documentary discussed the situation of akhdams in Yemen with focus on Saeeda's story calling for social action against such injustice.

Some mazaayina have also broken from the isolation and availed good education and are now working abroad in respectable jobs. In Yemen, they remain discriminated against regardless of their education or wealth but the trend is slowly changing.

Pakistan's Government Should Take Action to Protect Ahmadis

Human Rights Watch

Human Rights Watch (HRW) is an international organization founded to uphold human rights across the globe. In the following viewpoint, HRW argues that the minority religious group the Ahmadi is discriminated against in Pakistan. Ahmadi mosques have been destroyed, members of their community have been murdered, and Pakistani laws are specifically directed at preventing them from practicing their religious faith. In addition, according to HRW, Ahmadi homes and businesses are routinely robbed and destroyed.

As you read, consider the following questions:

1. What is the punishment for blasphemy under Pakistan's "Blasphemy Law"?
2. Approximately how many Ahmadis live in Pakistan?
3. When and where was the Ahmadiyya Muslim Community founded?

(New York)—Pakistan's federal and provincial governments should take immediate legal action against Islamist extremist groups responsible for threats and violence against the minority Ahmadiyya religious community, Human Rights Watch said today.

Human Rights Watch, "Pakistan: Massacre of Minority Ahmadis," www.hrw.org, June 1, 2010. Copyright © 2010 Human Rights Watch. Reprinted by permission.

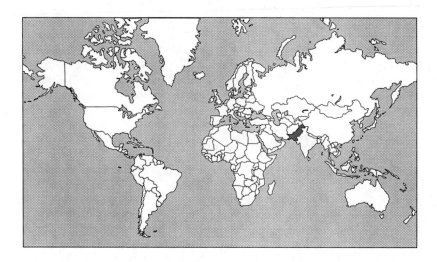

On May 28, 2010, extremist Islamist militants attacked two Ahmadiyya mosques in the central Pakistani city of Lahore with guns, grenades, and suicide bombs, killing 94 people and injuring well over a hundred. Twenty-seven people were killed at the Baitul Nur Mosque in the Model Town area of Lahore; 67 were killed at the Darul Zikr mosque in the suburb of Garhi Shahu. The Punjabi Taliban, a local affiliate of the Pakistani Taliban, called the Tehrik-e-Taliban Pakistan (TTP), claimed responsibility.

On the night of May 31, unidentified gunmen attacked the Intensive Care Unit of Lahore's Jinnah Hospital, where victims and one of the alleged attackers in Friday's attacks were under treatment, sparking a shoot-out in which at least a further 12 people, mostly police officers and hospital staff, were killed. The assailants succeeded in escaping.

"The mosque attacks and the subsequent attack on the hospital, amid rising sectarian violence, underscore the vulnerability of the Ahmadi community," said Ali Dayan Hasan, senior South Asia researcher at Human Rights Watch. "The government's failure to address religious persecution by Islamist groups effectively enables such atrocities."

The US Department of State annual report on human rights recorded the killing of 11 Ahmadis for their faith in 2009.

Human Rights Watch called on Pakistan's government to immediately introduce legislation in parliament to repeal laws discriminating against religious minorities such as the Ahmadis, including the penal statute that makes capital punishment mandatory for "blasphemy."

Human Rights Watch also urged the government of Punjab province, controlled by former prime minister Nawaz Sharif's Pakistan Muslim League (Nawaz) party, to investigate and prosecute as appropriate campaigns of intimidation, threats, and violence against the Ahmadiyya community by Islamist groups such as the Sunni Tehreek, Tehrik-e-Tahafaz-e-Naomoos-e-Risalat, Khatm-e-Nabuwat and other groups acting under the Taliban's umbrella. Leaders of these groups have frequently threatened to kill Ahmadis and attack the mosques where the killings took place. The anti-Ahmadiyya campaign has intensified in the past year, exemplified by the government allowing groups to place banners seeking the death of "Qadianis" (a derogatory term for Ahmadis) on the main thoroughfares of Lahore.

The anti-Ahmadiyya campaign has intensified in the past year.

The independent, nongovernmental Human Rights Commission of Pakistan (HRCP) and Ahmadi community leaders told Human Rights Watch that they had repeatedly brought these threats to the notice of Punjab Chief Minister Shahbaz Sharif, the provincial government, and the police controlled by the provincial authorities, and that they had asked for enhanced security for Ahmadiyya mosques given their vulnerability to attack. However, Human Rights Watch research found that the provincial government failed to act on the evidence or to ensure meaningful security to the mosques.

On May 30, Zaeem Qadri, advisor to Punjab Chief Minister Shahbaz Sharif, said in an interview on Dunya TV that the provincial government had failed to remove the threatening banners from the city's thoroughfares in order to prevent "adverse reaction against the government" by the groups responsible. On the same day, a Taliban statement "congratulated" Pakistanis for the attacks, calling people from the Ahmadiyya and Shia communities "the enemies of Islam and common people" and urging Pakistanis to take the "initiative" and kill every such person "in range."

"The Punjab government is either in denial about threats to Ahmadis and other minorities or is following a policy of willful discrimination," said Hasan. "The Punjab government's law enforcement authorities need to dispense with traditional prejudices and proactively protect heterodox communities like the Ahmadis, who now are in clear and serious danger from both the Taliban and sectarian militant groups historically supported by the state."

Founded in 1889 by Mirza Ghulam Ahmad, the Ahmadiyya community is a religious group that identifies itself as Muslim. Estimates suggest at least two million Ahmadis live in Pakistan. Ahmadis differ with other Muslims over the exact definition of Prophet Mohammed being the "final" monotheist prophet. Many Muslims consider the Ahmadiyya to be non-Muslims.

The persecution of the Ahmadiyya community is wholly legalized, even encouraged, by the Pakistani government. Pakistan's penal code explicitly discriminates against religious minorities and targets Ahmadis in particular by prohibiting them from "indirectly or directly posing as a Muslim." Ahmadis are prohibited from declaring or propagating their faith publicly, building mosques or even referring to them as such, or making the call for Muslim prayer.

Pakistan's "Blasphemy Law," as section 295-C of the Penal Code is known, makes the death penalty mandatory for blasphemy. Under this law, the Ahmadiyya belief in the prophethood of Mirza Ghulam Ahmad is considered blasphemous insofar as it "defiles the name of Prophet Mohammed." In 2009, at least 50 Ahmadis were charged under various provisions of the blasphemy law across Pakistan. Many of these individuals remain imprisoned.

Since the military government of Gen. Zia-ul-Haq unleashed a wave of persecution in the 1980s, violence against the Ahmadiyya community has never really ceased. Ahmadis continue to be killed and injured, and have their homes and businesses burned down in anti-Ahmadi attacks. The authorities continue to arrest, jail and charge Ahmadis for blasphemy and other offenses because of their religious beliefs. In several instances, the police have been complicit in harassment and the framing of false charges against Ahmadis, or stood by in the face of anti-Ahmadi violence.

The persecution of the Ahmadiyya community is wholly legalized, even encouraged, by the Pakistani government.

"Ahmadis unfortunately become easy targets in times of religious and political insecurity," said Hasan. "The Pakistani government has emboldened the extremists by failing to take action. It needs to repeal the laws used to persecute Ahmadis, and it must prosecute those responsible for anti-Ahmadi intimidation and violence."

However, the government seldom brings charges against perpetrators of anti-Ahmadi violence and discrimination. Research by Human Rights Watch indicates that the police have failed to apprehend anyone implicated in such activity in the last several years.

Since 2000, an estimated 400 Ahmadis have been formally charged in criminal cases, including blasphemy. Several have been convicted and face life imprisonment or death sentences pending appeal. The offenses charged included wearing an Islamic slogan on a shirt, planning to build an Ahmadi mosque in Lahore, and distributing Ahmadi literature in a public square. As a result, thousands of Ahmadis have fled Pakistan to seek asylum in countries including Canada and the United States.

Members of the Ahmadiyya community ("Ahmadis") profess to be Muslims.

Human Rights Watch said that the Pakistani government continues to actively encourage legal and procedural discrimination against Ahmadis. For example, all Pakistani Muslim citizens applying for passports are obliged to sign a statement explicitly stating that they consider the founder of the Ahmadi community an "imposter" and consider Ahmadis to be non-Muslims.

"Under Pakistan's Blasphemy Law, virtually any public act of worship or devotion by an Ahmadi can be treated as a criminal offense," said Hasan. "Ahmadis could be sentenced to death for simply professing their faith."

Human Rights Watch urged concerned governments and intergovernmental bodies to press the Pakistani government to:

- Repeal the Blasphemy Law;

- Prosecute those responsible for harassing, and planning and executing attacks against the Ahmadiyya and other minorities; and

- Take steps to encourage religious tolerance within Pakistani society.

"Pakistan's continued use of its blasphemy law against Ahamdis and other religious minorities is despicable," said

Hasan. "As long as such laws remain on the books, Pakistan will remain a laboratory for abuse in the name of religion."

Background on the Ahmadiyya Community

The Ahmadiyya Muslim Community, the official name of the community, is a contemporary messianic movement founded in 1889 by Mirza Ghulam Ahmad (1839–1908), who was born in the Punjabi village of Qadian, now in India. The relevant discriminatory laws in the Pakistani constitution and extremist Islamist groups derogatorily refer to the Ahmadiyya community as the "Qadiani" community, a term derived from the birthplace of the founder of the movement. In 1889, Ahmad declared that he had received divine revelation authorizing him to accept the baya'ah, or allegiance of the faithful. In 1891, he claimed to be the expected mahdi or messiah of the latter days, the "Awaited One" of the monotheist community of religions, and the messiah foretold by the Prophet Mohammed. Ahmad described his teachings, incorporating both Sufi and orthodox Islamic and Christian elements, as an attempt to revitalize Islam in the face of the British Raj, proselytizing Protestant Christianity, and resurgent Hinduism. Thus, the Ahmadiyya community believes that Ahmad conceived the community as a revivalist movement within Islam and not as a new religion.

Members of the Ahmadiyya community ("Ahmadis") profess to be Muslims. They contend that Ahmad meant to revive the true spirit and message of Islam that the Prophet Mohammed introduced and preached. Virtually all mainstream Muslim sects believe that Ahmad proclaimed himself as a prophet, thereby rejecting a fundamental tenet of Islam: Khatme Nabuwat (literally, the belief in the "finality of prophethood"—that the Prophet Mohammed was the last of the line of prophets leading back through Jesus, Moses, and Abraham). Ahmadis respond that Mirza Ghulam Ahmad was a non-law-bearing prophet subordinate in status to Prophet Mohammed; he came to illuminate and reform Islam, as predicted by Prophet Mohammed. For Ahmad and his followers, the Arabic Khatme Nabuwat does not refer to the finality of prophethood in a literal sense—that is, to prophethood's chronological cessation—but rather to its culmination and exemplification in the Prophet Mohammed. Ahmadis believe that "finality" in a chronological sense is a worldly concept, whereas "finality" in a metaphoric sense carries much more spiritual significance.

The exact size of the Ahmadiyya community worldwide is unclear, but estimates suggest they number under 10 million, mostly concentrated in India and Pakistan but also present in Bangladesh, Indonesia, Ghana, Burkina Faso, Gambia, Europe, and North America.

Background on the Persecution of the Ahmadiyya in Pakistan

The Ahmadiyya community has long been persecuted in Pakistan. Since 1953, when the first post-independence anti-Ahmadiyya riots broke out, the relatively small Ahmadi community in Pakistan has lived under threat. Between 1953 and 1973, this persecution was sporadic but, in 1974, a new wave of anti-Ahmadi disturbances spread across Pakistan. In response, Pakistan's parliament introduced amendments to the constitution which defined the term "Muslim" in the Pakistani context and listed groups that were deemed to be non-Muslim under Pakistani law. Put into effect on September 6, 1974, the amendment explicitly deprived Ahmadis of their identity as Muslims.

In 1984, Pakistan's penal code was amended yet again. As a result of these amendments, five ordinances that explicitly targeted religious minorities acquired legal status: a law against blasphemy; a law punishing the defiling of the Quran; a prohibition against insulting the wives, family, or companions of the Prophet of Islam; and two laws specifically restricting the activities of Ahmadis. On April 26, 1984, Gen. Mohammed Zia-ul-Haq issued these last two laws as part of Martial Law Ordinance XX, which amended Pakistan's Penal Code, sections 298-B and 298-C.

Ordinance XX undercut the activities of religious minorities generally, but struck at Ahmadis in particular by prohibiting them from "indirectly or directly posing as a Muslim." Ahmadis thus could no longer profess their faith, either orally or in writing. Pakistani police destroyed Ahmadi translations of and commentaries on the Quran and banned Ahmadi publications, the use of any Islamic terminology on Ahmadi wedding invitations, the offering of Ahmadi funeral prayers, and the displaying of the Kalima (the statement that "there is no god but Allah, Mohammed is Allah's prophet," the principal creed of Muslims) on Ahmadi gravestones. In addition, Ordinance XX prohibited Ahmadis from declaring their faith publicly, propagating their faith, building mosques, or making the call for Muslim prayer. In short, virtually any public act of worship or devotion by an Ahmadi could be treated as a criminal offense.

Since 1953 . . . the relatively small Ahmadi community in Pakistan has lived under threat. . . . In short, virtually any public act of worship or devotion by an Ahmadi could be treated as a criminal offense.

With the passage of the Criminal Law Act of 1986, parliament added section 295-C to the Pakistan Penal Code. The "Blasphemy Law," as it came to be known, made the death penalty mandatory for blasphemy. General Zia-ul-Haq and his military government institutionalized the persecution of Ahmadis as well as other minorities in Pakistan with section 295-C. The Ahmadi belief in the prophethood of Mirza Ghulam Ahmad was now considered blasphemous insofar as it "defiled the name of Prophet Mohammed." Therefore, theoretically, Ahmadis could be sentenced to death for simply professing their faith. Though the numbers vary from year to year, Ahmadis have been charged every year under the blasphemy laws since their introduction.

In 2009, at least 37 Ahmadis were charged under the general provisions of the Blasphemy Law and over 50 were charged under Ahmadi-specific provisions of the law. For example, in January 2009, five Ahmadis, including four children, were charged with blasphemy in Layyah district of Punjab province. The children were released after being jailed for six months. In July 2009, activists of the Sunni Tehreek, a militant group, staged protests until the local police in Faisalabad district of Punjab province agreed to register blasphemy cases against 32 Ahmadis for writing Quranic verses on the outer walls of their houses. The police registered cases against them under sections 295-A and 295-C. Throughout 2009, Ahmadi graveyards were threatened with desecration, and Ahmadi mosques continued to receive threats. In 2008, at least 15 Ahmadis were charged under various provisions of the Blasphemy Law. In addition to blasphemy charges, Ahmadis have sporadically come under physical attack. For example, in June 2006, a mob burned down Ahmadi shops and homes in Jhando Sahi village near the town of Daska in Punjab province, forcing more than 100 Ahmadis to flee. The police, though present at the scene, failed to intervene or arrest any of the culprits. However, the authorities charged seven Ahmadis under the Blasphemy Law. The Ahmadis subsequently returned to their homes. In October 2005, masked gunmen attacked Ahmadi worshippers in a mosque near the town of Mandi Bahauddin in Punjab province. Eight Ahmadis were killed and 18 injured in the attack. The perpetrators remain at large.

France's Burqa Ban Is a Boost for Equality

Greg Sheridan

In the following viewpoint, Greg Sheridan, foreign editor for the Australian, *argues that France's ban on the burqa (or burka) is a success for women's rights. He asserts that preventing women from wearing the traditional Muslim body covering in public places, such as in hospitals and schools, encourages equality. Although Sheridan acknowledges that the ban is targeted at Muslims, he insists that it is worthwhile because it allows for better integration into French society. He encourages governments in other countries to stand strong in favor of their own beliefs and customs.*

As you read, consider the following questions:

1. What is the difference between a hijab and a burqa?
2. When did France ban the hijab?
3. What are some other religious articles that cannot be worn in state schools in France?

Of all the countries of Europe, France has the best chance of coping successfully with large-scale Muslim immigration. That's not to say it's a very big chance, but it has some chance. This is because of France's strong republican ideology. This enables it to confer benefits as well as responsibilities on

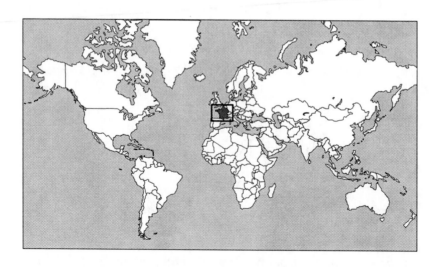

citizens regardless of ethnicity. French republicanism demands something of the citizen and asserts certain fundamental values.

Banning the Burka Is Liberating

This is most evident in the law banning the hijab, or Muslim headdress, from state schools. Last week [March 30, 2010] a French parliamentary committee recommended banning the full Muslim burka in government offices, public transport, hospitals and schools.[1]

The hijab is a bit more than a loose scarf that covers all the hair and generally the shoulders. The hijab reveals only the eyes and the burka covers everything, allowing a woman to see only through some sort of mesh arrangement. However, burka is the term most commonly used in the West to mean full face-covering, body length female Muslim attire.

France's President Nicolas Sarkozy has been the most effective Western statesman on these issues. He gave an eloquent speech last year in which he rejected the burka and said it offends French values. This was not primarily because of the

1. The burka (or burqa) was banned by the French government on September 14, 2010.

distance and separation the burka enforces between its wearer and the broader society. Rather, it was because of women's rights.

When, in 2005, the French banned the hijab, I thought they were making a mistake. Broadly speaking, I don't really care what anybody wears. But I was wrong. Spending time in France last year, I realised the French see this as a great liberal reform in the interests of women's rights. The French go to great lengths to distinguish secular from religious spaces. They have gone to great lengths to make this law non-discriminatory. At state schools, Christians cannot wear large crosses, Jews cannot wear yarmulkes, Sikhs cannot wear turbans.

The truth is this law was aimed at Muslims. And everyone knows this. One consequence of large-scale Muslim immigration, therefore, is that all of France has to become a little less liberal, in that Christians, Jews and Sikhs must suffer restrictions when there was no problem at all in their religious dress. But the hijab is both a symbol and a tool of the repression of women. The reform has been such a success because for several hours each day, young Muslim women at state schools are French women, with the rights and independence and respect that accrue to French women. They are for that time no longer subject to the rules of their brothers and fathers and the religious extremists in their communities.

Incidentally, the French rules are similar to those that have applied in Turkey for much of its modern history.

The truth is this law was aimed at Muslims.

Living Up to French Values

But the most important aspect of the French law is that it makes explicit to the Muslim minority the demand that to be a French citizen you must subscribe to, and live up to, certain

French civic values, of which equality for women is one. The proposed limited ban on the burka is an extension of this. And here is a perplexing conundrum. If you really believe that women, but not men, should be fully covered, why would you want to live in a society such as France, or indeed Australia, in the first place?

Here we meet a hard truth of Muslim immigration to Europe, and perhaps to Australia. There is a strong body of belief that at least a large number of the African, and especially Maghrebi, Muslims who move to Europe do so not to embrace the European lifestyle, that is to pay the immigrant's traditional compliment to the new society, but to recreate their Third World lifestyle at a European standard of living.

Diversity is a good thing and there is a vast range of values and traditions that are perfectly acceptable in most Western societies. But women's inherent inequality is not one of them.

Muslim immigration to Australia and the US has so far been much more successful than Muslim immigration to Europe. This is often seen to be a consequence of our superior settlement policies, in particular that the US not only confers rights on immigrants but imposes civic obligations on them as well. The truth might be that it is just because the relative numbers of Muslims in the US and Australia are so much smaller.

Mass Muslim immigration challenges a liberal Western society in a way that no previous immigration did, in part because most mainstream interpretations of Islam see it as requiring its adherents to establish a political order as well as a religious order. The vast majority of Australian Muslims are perfectly law abiding, happy with the Australian civic order and in every way good citizens. But the experience of Europe strongly suggests this could be quite different if the Muslim minority were much, much larger.

For societies such as Australia and the US, the traditional pro-immigration bias, which I wholly share, may need some calibration in relation to Muslim immigration. Successful immigration involves acceptance and immersion in the core values of the new society. A state that tolerates open and socially destructive defiance of this is very weak.

Mass Muslim immigration challenges a liberal Western society in a way that no previous immigration did.

These are very sensitive issues. But Western civilisation needs to stand for some positive values beyond an anything-goes relativism that will be destroyed by more vigorous belief systems.

The French are moving cautiously, incrementally, and in my view belatedly, but with almost unique courage and intelligence, to try to repair the outcome of the nihilistic trends in Western intellectual life and their interplay with a mass immigration that Europeans did not choose and have never understood. Vive la France!

Burqa Bans Smother Europe's Civil Liberties

Mehdi Hasan

Mehdi Hasan is senior editor (politics) of the New Statesman. In the following viewpoint excerpt, Hasan argues that banning the burqa (or burka), a traditional whole-body covering for Muslim women, targets just a few Muslim women but is a violation of their civil right to dress as they please without state interference as well as of their freedom of religion. He notes that such bans will likely backfire because they run counter to their professed objective by putting women in prison in an effort to free them from aspects of cultural oppression and by causing a repressed minority to respond by becoming more entrenched in its practices.

As you read, consider the following questions:

1. How many women are likely to wear the veil in Belgium? In France?

2. According to Hasan, what did French President Nicolas Sarkozy say about the burqa?

3. According to Hasan, what seems to be the primary driving force behind the moves in various countries to ban the burqa?

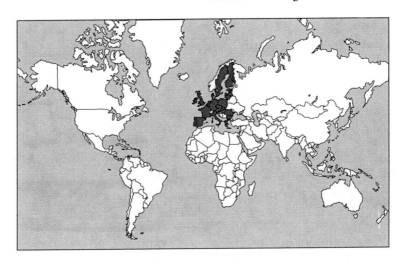

It has been condemned as sinister, frightening, misogynistic and oppressive. Indeed, nothing seems to provoke more suspicion of Europe's 15 million Muslims than the face veil worn by a tiny minority of women. Even many followers of Islam are keen to disown and denounce it. In heated discussions with my own father over the past few weeks, I discovered that he is one of those who take a sterner line, describing the face veil as "un-Islamic and unnecessary".

"If not for anything else," he told me, "it should be banned for security reasons." I am no fan of the face veil, but I disagree with Dad. Moves to ban it will surely backfire.

In recent months, several European governments have begun to legislate restrictions on both the niqab, a face veil that leaves the area around the eyes clear and is usually combined with a full body covering, and the burqa, which covers the entire face and body, leaving just a mesh screen to see through. On 29 April, Belgium became the first European country to impose a nationwide ban on wearing a full face veil in public. . . .

Anyone found flouting the new law, which will come into force after Belgium's general election on 13 June, will face a fine of up to €25 (£21) and possibly seven days in jail. For

Fouad Lahssaini, a Green MP in Belgium who emigrated there from Morocco as a youth, passing a ban on the face veil is like "taking out a bazooka to kill a fly".

About 215 women "at most" in Belgium wear the veil, according to Edouard Delruelle, co-director of the Belgian Institute for Equal Opportunities. Others put the number as low as 30, out of an estimated Muslim population of just over 600,000 and a total Belgian population of 10.8 million. Most Belgians will never meet a niqab-clad woman.

For Fouad Lahssaini, a Green MP in Belgium who emigrated there from Morocco as a youth, passing a ban on the face veil is like "taking out a bazooka to kill a fly".

It's a similar story in other European countries, but the anti-burqa cause is spreading. France, Italy and the Netherlands are also considering nationwide bans. The French security services estimate that 2,000 of the roughly two million adult Muslim women in France—0.1 per cent—wear the full face veil, and a third of them are thought to be converts to Islam. Yet the French are planning "emergency legislation" to ban the burqa and niqab before the country's legislators go on their summer holiday in August. The National Assembly has passed a non-binding resolution condemning the face veil as "an affront to the nation's values of dignity and equality", and the French cabinet has approved a bill making it illegal to wear clothing designed to cover the face in public.

The penalties in France will be much higher than in Belgium. The fine for a first offence will be €150 (£130). And a man who is found to have forced a woman to wear a full-length veil by "violence or threats" will be punished with a fine of €15,000 and face imprisonment. The crackdown on the veil has come from the very top of the political establishment, with President Nicolas Sarkozy declaring that the burqa is "not welcome" in France and denouncing it as a symbol of female "subservience and debasement".

Such has been the hysteria that French politicians and pundits have whipped up over the veil that the country has been hit by "burqa rage". On 15 May, a Muslim woman leaving a shoe shop in Trignac, near Saint-Nazaire on the west coast of France, is said to have overheard a 60-year-old woman lawyer making "snide remarks about her black burqa". The 26-year-old Muslim convert later described to reporters how "things got nasty. The older woman grabbed my veil to the point of ripping it off." The two women allegedly traded blows before being separated by shop assistants and were then arrested by the police.

An officer close to the case said: "The lawyer said she was not happy seeing a fellow shopper wearing a veil and wanted the ban introduced as soon as possible." She is also said to have likened the Muslim woman to Belphegor, a mythical demon who frequently covers up his hideous features using a mask.

So much for a secular state protecting religious freedom. Yet the proposed ban may, in fact, be unconstitutional. The Council of State, France's highest legal and administrative authority, warned in March that "a general and absolute ban on the full veil as such can have no incontestable judicial basis", and that it could be rejected by the courts for violating both national law and the European Convention on Human Rights. . . .

So, why pursue it? Polls suggest that a ban is popular, and Sarkozy's personal poll rating is at an all-time low. For François Hollande, the former head of the French Socialist Party, "the tactic is clear. It's about getting back a hold of a part of the electorate which has in part retreated into abstention or voting for the far right."

Yet support for a ban cuts across the left-right divide. In Belgium, the idea was first proposed by the Flemish far right;

in France, it was pushed by a communist mayor. On the right, the veil is seen as a threat to European and in particular Christian culture; a symbol of a foreign, belligerent faith community, the "other"—even though few Muslim women wear it.

On the left, it is seen as a repressive garment that subjugates women and violates their rights. Yet not every Muslim woman is forced, under threat of violence, to wear the veil by a husband, father or brother; some wear the niqab or burqa as a matter of choice.

Despite the ban being sold by both left and right as a measure to liberate oppressed Muslim women, it is opposed by leading human rights groups. "At a time when Muslims in Europe feel more vulnerable than ever, the last thing needed is a ban like this," said Judith Sunderland of Human Rights Watch on 21 April. "Treating pious Muslim women like criminals won't help integrate them." The irony of using the threat of prison to freewomen from the so-called prison of the burqa is not lost on Muslim commentators, either. "The Belgians have a funny idea of liberation," says the British Muslim writer and activist Myriam François-Cerrah: "criminalising women in order to free them."

Amnesty International has condemned the Belgian move as "an attack on religious freedom", and Sunderland has said that "restrictions on women wearing the veil in public life are as much a violation of the rights of women as is forcing them to wear a veil". The award-winning Iranian graphic novelist Marjane Satrapi, an outspoken critic of the veil, agrees. "It is surely a basic human right that someone can choose what she wears without interference from the state," she wrote in 2003. . . .

I am not defending the face veil. I agree with the 100 or so imams and Muslim religious advisers from 40 different countries at a recent conference in Vienna organised by the Islamic Religious Authority in Austria, who concluded that Islam does not make it a requirement for women to wear face veils. After all, the face veil is mentioned nowhere in the Quran, nor is there a Quranic injunction to cover the face. . . .

As the hijab-wearing British Muslim writer Fareena Alam pointed out in 2006, the controversy over the veil "has more to do with Europe's own identity crisis than with the presence of some 'dangerous other'".

My own Muslim wife, of Indian origin but born and brought up in the United States, wears a headscarf (but not a face veil). She made the decision to wear the hijab at the age of 25, and it was a spiritual, not a political or cultural choice. I accept that, for many Muslim women, covering their face is not a choice, but is a ban the best response? There are many reasons to believe it is self-defeating.

For a start, state-imposed bans will poison relations between Muslims and non-Muslims even further. Bans often encourage defiance. In the words of the atheist writer Shikha Dalmia, of the Los Angeles-based Reason Foundation, "this law can't help but inflame French Muslims, not encourage them to assimilate. Besieged minorities after all tighten—not loosen—their grip on their ways.". . .

Most damningly, there is early evidence that a ban on the face veil could serve further to isolate and seclude the marginalised Muslim women whom it is supposed to help liberate. In Italy, at the end of April, Tunisian-born Amel Marmouri became the first woman to be fined for wearing a face veil when she was stopped outside a post office in the city of Novara. Marmouri was fined €500—and her husband has said he will now ensure she stays at home so that she never again has to venture out without her veil. . . .

In truth, the moves towards a ban seem primarily driven by a fear of Islam, the fastest-growing faith on the continent, and an inability on the part of Muslims and non-Muslims alike to discuss the future of Islam in Europe calmly. As the hijab-wearing British Muslim writer Fareena Alam pointed out in 2006, the controversy over the veil "has more to do with Europe's own identity crisis than with the presence of some 'dangerous other'. At a time when post-communist, secular, democratic Europe was supposed to have been ascendant, playing its decisive role at the end of history, Islam came and spoiled the party."

Or, as Isabel Soumaya, a convert to Islam and vice-president of the Association of Belgian Muslims, put it in an interview with the *Washington Post* on 15 May, Europe's politicians are "preying on voters' fears". The veil ban, she said, "is racism and a form of Islamophobia".

Periodical Bibliography

The following articles have been selected to supplement the diverse views presented in this chapter.

Yasemin Akbaba — "Who Discriminates More? Comparing Religious Discrimination in Western Democracies, Asia and the Middle East," *Civil Wars*, vol. 11, no. 3, September 2009.

Geoffrey Alderman — "We Jews Cannot Have It Both Ways," *Jerusalem Post*, November 16, 2009.

China Post — "Taiwan Needs to Cultivate a Politically Correct Culture," October 1, 2010.

Zaki Cooper — "Faith and Business: A New Deal for the Modern Workplace," *Times* (London), September 27, 2008.

Michael B. Farrell — "Fired from Hollister for Wearing the Hijab," *Christian Science Monitor*, February 26, 2010.

Eric Lichtblau — "Questions Raised Anew About Religion in Military," *New York Times*, February 28, 2009.

Mail Online (UK) — "Muslim Woman Sacked for Refusing to Wear a Headscarf," October 3, 2010.

Lisa Pryor — "Religion Is Fine as Long as It's Muslim or It's Democrat," *Australian*, January 26, 2009.

Washington Times — "When Religious Discrimination Is Vital," December 1, 2010.

Richelle Wiseman — "It Is Not Bigoted for Canadians to Confront Honour Killings," *Gazette* (Montreal), September 16, 2010.

For Further Discussion

Chapter 1

1. The authors in this chapter explore the impact of health discrimination on the well-being of the world's citizens. Do you think there are any justifiable reasons to discriminate against people based on their health status? Using the viewpoints in this chapter, explain your answer.

Chapter 2

1. According to the authors in this chapter, what are the consequences of discriminating against people based on their gender or sexuality? What should be done to prevent these kinds of discrimination? Explain your answers.

Chapter 3

1. After reading the viewpoints in this chapter, do you think racial and ethnic discrimination exist around the world? If so, what should be done to prevent these kinds of discrimination? Use the viewpoints to support your answers.

Chapter 4

1. Do you agree that the examples the authors present in this chapter are instances of religious and cultural discrimination? Explain your reasoning.

Organizations to Contact

The editors have compiled the following list of organizations concerned with the issues debated in this book. The descriptions are derived from materials provided by the organizations. All have publications or information available for interested readers. The list was compiled on the date of publication of the present volume; the information provided here may change. Be aware that many organizations take several weeks or longer to respond to inquiries, so allow as much time as possible.

Amnesty International (AI)
1 Easton Street, London   WC1X 0DW
   United Kingdom
44-20-74135500 • fax: 44-20-79561157
website: www.amnesty.org

Amnesty International (AI) conducts research and generates action to prevent and end grave abuses of human rights and to demand justice for those whose rights have been violated. AI members and supporters exert influence on governments, political bodies, companies, and intergovernmental groups and take up human rights issues by mobilizing public pressure through mass demonstrations, vigils, and direct lobbying. The AI website offers an extensive number of publications, including "Mexico: Journeys of Hope and Fear" and "China: Fear of Disappearance of Activist and Family."

Association for Women's Rights in Development (AWID)
215 Spadina Avenue, Suite 150, Toronto, Ontario   M5T 2C7
   Canada
416 594 3773 • fax: 416 594 0330
e-mail: contact@awid.org
website: www.awid.org

The Association for Women's Rights in Development (AWID) is an international, multigenerational, feminist, creative, future-orientated membership organization committed to achieving gender equality, sustainable development, and women's human rights. AWID members are researchers, academics, students, educators, activists, business people, policy makers, development practitioners, funders, and more. AWID offers a number of publications through its website, including investigative reports such as "A Brand New Constitution, but Can Women Enjoy Land Rights?" and "Forced and Arranged Marriages: Between Elucidation and Scandalizing Distortion."

Child Rights Information Network (CRIN)
East Studio, 2, Pontypool Place, London   SE1 8QF
  United Kingdom
44-20-7401-2257
e-mail: info@crin.org
website: www.crin.org

Inspired by the United Nations Convention on the Rights of the Child, the Child Rights Information Network (CRIN) is building a global network for children's rights. Through advocacy campaigns and international children's rights coalitions, CRIN strives to make existing human rights enforcement mechanisms accessible for all. The CRIN website provides information about children's rights in countries across the globe and provides access to its investigative reports, including "Children in Haiti—One Year After" and "Realizing Children's Rights."

Equal Rights Trust (ERT)
126 North End Road, London   W14 9PP
  United Kingdom
44-(0)207 610 2786 • fax: 44-(0)203 441 7436
e-mail: info@equalrightstrust.org
website: www.equalrightstrust.org

The Equal Rights Trust (ERT) is an independent international organization with a purpose of combating discrimination and promoting equality as a fundamental human right and a basic principle of social justice. Established as an advocacy organization, resource center, and think tank, it focuses on the complex and complementary relationship between different types of discrimination and developing strategies for translating the principles of equality into practice. In addition to statements of principle, the ERT website includes many resources, including *The Equal Rights Review*.

Gay and Lesbian Alliance Against Defamation (GLAAD)
5455 Wilshire Boulevard, Suite 1500, Los Angeles, CA   90036
(323) 933-2240 • fax: (323) 933-2241
website: www.glaad.org

The Gay and Lesbian Alliance Against Defamation (GLAAD) amplifies the voice of the lesbian, gay, bisexual, and transgender (LGBT) community by empowering real people to share their stories, holding the media accountable for the words and images they present, and helping grassroots organizations communicate effectively. By ensuring that the stories of LGBT people are heard through the media, GLAAD promotes understanding, increases acceptance, and advances equality. In addition to position papers, GLAAD's website offers several media guides, including *GLAAD College Media Reference Guide* for college journalists who wish to write about LGBT issues.

International Association for Religious Freedom (IARF)
3-8-21 Sangenya-Nishi, Taisho-ku, Osaka   551-0001
   Japan
81-(0)675 035 602
e-mail: hq@iarf.net
website: www.iarf.net

The International Association for Religious Freedom (IARF) is a United Kingdom–based charity working for freedom of religion and belief at a global level. Founded in 1900, IARF encourages interfaith dialogue and tolerance with member groups in twenty-five countries from faith traditions including Buddhism, Christianity, Hinduism, Islam, Shinto, and Zoroastrianism. The IARF website offers reports on its recent projects and newsletters such as the *Religious Freedom Young Adult Network Bulletin*.

International Disability Alliance (IDA)

WCC Building, nos. 153–154, 150 route de Ferney
Geneva   1211
  Switzerland
website: www.internationaldisabilityalliance.org

Established in 1999, the International Disability Alliance (IDA) is the network of global and regional organizations of persons with disabilities that promotes the effective implementation of the United Nations Convention on the Rights of Persons with Disabilities. IDA was instrumental in establishing the International Disability Caucus (IDC), which is the network of global, regional, and national organizations of persons with disabilities and allied nongovernmental organizations. IDA publishes the *Disability Rights Bulletin* each month.

International Movement Against All Forms of Discrimination and Racism (IMADR)

3-5-11, Roppongi, Minato-ku, Tokyo   106-0032
  Japan
(81-3) 3586-7447 • fax: (81-3) 3586-7462
e-mail: imadris@imadr.org
website: www.imadr.org

The International Movement Against All Forms of Discrimination and Racism (IMADR) is an international nonprofit, nongovernmental human rights organization devoted to eliminating discrimination and racism, forging international solidarity among discriminated minorities, and advancing the international human rights system. Founded in 1988 by one of Japan's largest minorities, the Buraku people, IMADR has grown to be a global network of concerned individuals and minority groups with regional committees and partners in Asia, Europe, North America, and Latin America. IMADR's newsletter, *Connect*, and journal, *People's for Human Rights*, are available through its website.

UNAIDS

20 Avenue Appia, Geneva   1211
  Switzerland
website: www.unaids.org

UNAIDS, the Joint United Nations Programme on HIV/AIDS, is an innovative partnership that leads and inspires the world in achieving universal access to HIV prevention, treatment, care, and support. UNAIDS fulfills its mission by speaking out in solidarity with the people most affected by HIV in defense of human dignity, human rights, and gender equality, and supporting inclusive country leadership for sustainable responses that are integral to and integrated with national health and development efforts.

UNICEF

United States Fund for UNICEF, 125 Maiden Lane
11th Floor, New York, NY   10038
(212) 686-5522 • fax: (212) 779-1679
website: www.unicef.org

Mandated by the United Nations General Assembly, UNICEF—the United Nations Children's Fund—is an international organization developed to support the needs of children, including discrimination against young people. In addition to serving as advocates for the world's most needy, UNICEF works with legislature to shape global policies involving equality and compassion for children. In addition to its annual report, UNICEF regularly publishes the *State of the World's Children* and *Progress for Children*.

United Nations Educational, Scientific and Cultural Organization (UNESCO)

7, place de Fontenoy 75352, Paris   07 SP
  France
33 (0)1 45 68 10 00
website: www.unesco.org

United Nations Educational, Scientific and Cultural Organization (UNESCO) contributes to the fight against racism and discrimination through research and outreach programs and projects. UNESCO participated in the World Conference Against Racism, Racial Discrimination, Xenophobia and Related Intolerance in Durban, South Africa, in 2001. In addition to interviews with persons important in the fight against global discrimination, the UNESCO website also provides links to many of the organization's statements, including "Strengthening the Fight Against Racism and Discrimination."

World Federation of the Deafblind (WFDB)
Snehvidevej 13, Noerresundby   DK-9400
   Denmark
45 98 19 20 99 • fax: 45 98 19 20 57
website: www.wfdb.org

The World Federation of the Deafblind (WFDB) represents national organizations of individuals who are deaf and blind, and advocates for the rights of such individuals. It disseminates information about "deafblindness" and the services that deaf and blind people need to lead independent lives. The WFDB website provides forums for persons seeking more information about international issues concerning deaf and blind people and links to its position statements.

Bibliography of Books

Martha R. Bireda *Cultures in Conflict: Eliminating Racial Profiling.* Lanham, MD: Rowman and Littlefield Education, 2010.

Nicky ten Bokum, et al., eds. *Age Discrimination Law in Europe.* Alphen aan den Rijn, The Netherlands: Kluwer Law International, 2009.

Deborah L. Brake *Getting in the Game: Title IX and the Women's Sports Revolution.* New York: New York University Press, 2010.

Ronald C. Brown *Understanding Labor and Employment Law in China.* Cambridge: Cambridge University Press, 2010.

Kingsley Browne *Co-Ed Combat: The New Evidence That Women Shouldn't Fight the Nation's Wars.* New York: Sentinel, 2007.

Reginald Anthony Byron *Disposable Workers: Race, Gender, and Firing Discrimination.* Columbus: Ohio State University, 2009.

Miguel Angel Centeno and Katherine S. Newman, eds. *Discrimination in an Unequal World.* Oxford: Oxford University Press, 2010.

Prem Chowdhry, ed. *Gender Discrimination in Land Ownership.* New Delhi, India: Sage Publications, 2009.

Robert L. Dipboye and Adrienne Colella, eds.	*Discrimination at Work: The Psychological and Organizational Bases.* Mahwah, NJ: Lawrence Erlbaum Associates, 2005.
Joel Wm. Friedman, ed.	*Employment Discrimination Stories.* New York: Foundation Press, 2006.
Roland G. Fryer Jr.	*Racial Inequality in the 21st Century: The Declining Significance of Discrimination.* Cambridge, MA: National Bureau of Economic Research, 2010.
Deborah Hellman	*When Is Discrimination Wrong?* Cambridge, MA: Harvard University Press, 2008.
Human Rights Watch	*Discrimination in the Name of Neutrality: Headscarf Bans for Teachers and Civil Servants in Germany.* New York, 2009.
Marshall B. Kapp	*Legal Aspects of Elder Care.* Sudbury, MA: Jones and Bartlett Publishers, 2010.
Spencer Keen and Richard Oulton	*Disability Discrimination in Employment.* Oxford: Oxford University Press, 2009.
Bankim Chandra Mandal	*Protective Discrimination Policy: In Search of Equality.* Delhi: Abhijeet Publications, 2009.
Errol P. Mendes and Sakunthula Srighanthan, eds.	*Confronting Discrimination and Inequality in China: Chinese and Canadian Perspectives.* Ottawa: University of Ottawa Press, 2009.

Hugo Ñopo, Alberto Chong, Andrea Moro, eds. *Discrimination in Latin America: An Economic Perspective.* Washington, DC: Inter-American Development Bank: World Bank, 2010.

Bertha M.N. Ochieng and Carl L.A. Hylton, eds. *Black Families in Britain as the Site of Struggle.* Manchester: Manchester University Press, 2010.

Navtej K. Purewal *Son Preference: Sex Selection, Gender and Culture in South Asia.* Oxford, UK: Berg, 2010.

Barbara Kate Repa *Your Rights in the Workplace.* Berkeley, CA: Nolo, 2002.

Deborah L. Rhode *The Beauty Bias: The Injustice of Appearance in Life and Law.* New York: Oxford University Press, 2010.

Robert S. Rycroft *The Economics of Inequality, Discrimination, Poverty, and Mobility.* Armonk, NY: M.E. Sharpe, 2009.

Anne Stangl, et al. *Tackling HIV-Related Stigma and Discrimination in South Asia.* Washington, DC: World Bank, 2010.

Sukhadeo Thorat and Katherine S. Newman, eds. *Blocked by Caste: Economic Discrimination in Modern India.* New Delhi: Oxford University Press, 2010.

Lucy Vickers *Religious Freedom, Religious Discrimination, and the Workplace.* Portland, OR: Hart, 2008.

Bernard E. Whitley Jr. and Mary E. Kite *The Psychology of Prejudice and Discrimination.* Belmont, CA: Thomson Wadsworth, 2006.

Index

Geographic headings and page numbers in **boldface** refer to viewpoints about that country or region.